THE ART AND SCIENCE OF BOOK PUBLISHING

THE ART AND SCIENCE OF BOOK PUBLISHING

by

HERBERT S. BAILEY, JR.

OHIO UNIVERSITY PRESS

ATHENS

Library of Congress Cataloging-in-Publication Data

Bailey, Herbert Smith.
The art and science of book publishing /
by Herbert S. Bailey, Jr.–3rd ed.
p. cm.
Includes bibliographical references.
ISBN 0-8214-0970-0 (paperback)
1. Publishers and publishing–Management.
2. Book industries and trade–Management. I Title.
Z278.B15 1990 90-7103
070.5'068–DC20 CIP

Ohio University Press edition first published 1990
10 09 08 07 06 05 04 03 02 9 8 7 6 5 4

Printed in the United States of America

Ohio University Press books are printed on acid-free paper ∞
This book is printed on recycled paper

To Betty and our children
John
Jim
Robin
and George

CONTENTS

PREFACE

This discussion of management in publishing, while attempting to be analytic and objective, is really a very personal book. It represents my own struggles, after years as an editor, to learn to manage a publishing house—a struggle that is still going on after more than fifteen years as director of Princeton University Press. The ideas presented here are not intended to explain what is widely done in publishing, though many references are made to general practice. They are meant to focus analytically on the problems of management: organization, communication, external and internal relationships, types of decisions, work flow, personnel, finances, planning, new technologies, and so forth. Certain large topics in publishing, such as copyright, are omitted entirely as not being appropriate to my purpose. Still, I hope the book will be as useful to others as the writing of it has been to me.

In a sense, work on the book really began in 1954 when, with new responsibilities in publishing, I knew I had to get better control of operating costs and improve our methods of setting print orders and prices. At that time I worked out the method of allocating operating costs described in Chapter IV, and we have used it at Princeton with success and satisfaction ever since. In the summer of 1967, having become increasingly aware of "growing pains" in our publishing house, I wrote a long memorandum on organization and communication that essentially constitutes Chapter II. At the same time I began reading in the fields of operations research and management science, and we experienced at the Press a shortage of working capital which required study of inventory and reprint policies. This led in the fall of 1967 to the studies of optimum quantities to print, described in Chapter IV. These studies were continued in 1968, and in their very nature will go on indefinitely as a systematic means of feeding experience into the decision-making process. The chapter on new technologies is adapted with few changes from an article in the June 11, 1966, issue of the *Saturday Review*, with the kind permission of the publisher. A leave, generously granted by the trustees of the Press, permitted me to complete a draft of the manuscript in the summer of 1968. I am grateful for that opportunity.

This preface gives me an occasion to thank various people not so much for help with the book but for what they have taught me about publishing. Some of them may even want to disown the book, finding its approach uncongenial, but I would not want to fail to acknowledge my debt to them. First I want to thank the trustees of Princeton University Press not only for their support over the years but particularly for the occasions when they have questioned, modified, or even disapproved proposals from the administration. Such experiences have been especially instructive. I owe a lot of my education in publishing to the publisher-members of our trustees: Mr. Charles Scribner, Jr., of Scribner's, who would have been a superb mathematician or classicist if he had not been destined to become the most distinguished publisher in the Scribner line; Mr. Raymond C. Harwood, formerly of Harper & Row, certainly one of the best financial experts in publishing; Mr. Henry A. Laughlin of Houghton-Mifflin, a dedicated publisher with an extraordinary knowledge of printing; Mr. Harold W. McGraw, Jr., of McGraw-Hill, a member of another distinguished publishing dynasty, with his keen knowledge of marketing; and Mr. Novell B. Samuels, from whom I learned so much during the fourteen years when we were colleagues at Princeton University Press and during his subsequent term as president of the American Book Company. In the first chapter of this book I have emphasized the importance of enthusiasm and a sense of books and their readers; no one has these qualities in greater degree than Mr. Datus C. Smith, Jr., who hired me for my first publishing job and who later, as president of Franklin Book Programs, did so much to inspire and instruct publishers in many countries where publishing hardly existed.

The trustees of Princeton University Press include several representatives of the university administration to whom I feel a debt: Dean J. Douglas Brown, Sir Hugh Taylor, and Mr. Ricardo A. Mestres. It would be inappropriate for me to recite here the many members of the Prinecton faculty who have served on our Editorial Board and who have helped to guide our editorial decisions toward scholarly objectives, but I want to name one, Professor Jacob Viner, renowned economist, who was chairman of the Editorial Board when I assumed the duties of editor; he taught me a number of sometimes painful lessons about standards of scholarship. My thanks go to another economist, Professor Jesse Markham of the Harvard Business School, who read the manuscript and made a number of helpful suggestions. I also wish to thank Daniel Melcher, until recently President of the R. R. Bowker Co., for his careful reading and detailed comments on the manuscript.

With deepest gratitude, I want to acknowledge the contributions of the Press staff to my own thinking on many occasions. As I have tried to emphasize in Chapter II, the interaction of the staff is a continuing process in which everyone, including the publisher, is constantly contributing and learning. My debts to staff members are many, but I want particularly to acknowledge what I owe to our associate director and editor, Miss R. Miriam Brokaw, and to our associate director and controller, Mr. William C. Becker, two extraordinarily able and versatile publishers. And for her unfailing common sense and wonderful human qualities (to say nothing of her typing this manuscript), I want to thank my secretary, Mrs. George F. Brown.

It has been an interesting experience to sit on the *other* side of the editorial table. The people at Harper & Row have been most understanding and helpful; I told them that for this book I would try to act like an author and not like a publisher. Nahum Waxman has been an intelligent and tactful editor of a book on a subject which he knows as well as the author, and in which the author's views are not always orthodox.

This book is dedicated to my wife and children, who have so often shared my struggles with the problems discussed, and who by their presence have provided a constant reminder that human considerations are more important than technical or financial ones.

Herbert S. Bailey, Jr.

January, 1970

PREFACE TO THE OHIO UNIVERSITY PRESS EDITION

When Duane Schneider, director of Ohio University Press, expressed an interest in reissuing *The Art and Science of Book Publishing*, he generously suggested that I might want to do a thorough revision, since the book was first published twenty years ago. It was a tempting idea, but I decided not to revise for two reasons: first, so many local features of the publishing landscape have changed that very extensive rewriting would be required; and second and more important, the basic principles of publishing have not changed, so at heart the book is as good as it ever was. This preface aims to add some contemporary perspective to the original text as a guide to the reader of the 1990s.

This is a book about publishing management—about how a publishing house works and how the various activities may be controlled and coordinated. It does not provide detailed information about editing or designing or manufacturing or marketing or fulfillment or accounting, though it deals with all these subjects, and it should help anyone working in any of these activities.

In discussing publishing management there is too much tendency to assume that all books are alike. All books are *not* alike;

even all books in a narrow field or category are not alike, and if they are treated alike, something is lost. Each book is the unique creation of its author and is itself unique.

But in some ways all books *are* alike. The same set of decisions must be made for each book with respect to acceptance, contract stipulations, editing, and so forth, on to marketing, reprinting, and eventually letting the book go out of print or remaindering. In making those decisions the publisher must draw on his experience with *similar* books, for there are similarities even among unique objects. This book is intended to help identify those decisions and show how experience may be brought to bear in producing better decisions.

The considerations going into those decisions are not different from what they were twenty years ago, but today it is much easier to bring experience to bear in a systematic way. The computer has made it simple to assemble information for decisions on print orders, pricing, discounting, reprinting, inventory control, cash flow, and so forth. In the 1970 edition computers are hardly mentioned; indeed hand calculators were just coming in at that time, and at one point I even mentioned the slide rule! But today every publisher can easily have, for example, computer-generated up-to-date historical sales reports by subject category (or other categories) with average discounts, rate-of-sale curves, price-per-page analyses, and the like. This book indicates, especially in Chapter IV and the Appendix, what kind of information is needed and how it may be used.

If I were rewriting the book today I would remove a good many of the mathematical equations. To me, in the writing, they helped to clarify relationships, and I hoped they would do that for others, but I have learned that even simple formulas scare some readers. The reasoning behind the equations is all in the text, and I hope that mathophobic readers will just skip the equations. My object was *not* to reduce publishing to a mathematical science; it is not and never can be that—thank goodness! The publisher's role as the link between the author and the reader, who are *not* mathematical entities, guarantees that. And that's what makes publishing interesting. It requires judgment and enterprise and taste—and intelligent management.

While writing the book I coined the term "micropublishing" to mean the process of publishing a single title, as contrasted with "macropublishing," meaning the activity of the whole publishing firm. I did not anticipate that the word "micropublishing" would later be used as the name of the part of the publishing industry that publishes in "microform." If I had, I would have used another term in Chapter IV. I hope readers will not be confused by the special use of the term here.

Costs and prices in the examples in this book will seem very low to readers in the 1990s. Inflation has taken its toll, and I make no apology for that. Substitute contemporary figures and make the calculations. The reasoning still applies.

To some this may seem a "heavy" book, but I hope it also conveys the challenge and excitement and satisfactions that can come from successful management. No publishing house, however great its authors and editors, can afford to ignore the problems of management. A well-managed house can publish better books more successfully. Houses with superb lists have failed because of bad management. Contemplating this phenomenon I long ago composed the following two poems, which originally appeared in the *Publishers' Weekly* and have since been reprinted in various accounting textbooks. I offer them here as a fitting way to end this Preface.

THE BOTTOM LINE

The bottom line, it seems to me,
Is just a huge calamity.
It's all my boss can ever see—
That bottom line.

The bottom line, it's all in all.
It must be large and black, *not* small
Or red. Red ink is gall
   On the bottom line.

Red ink sends chills along my spine.
Red ink is wormwood in my wine.
Red ink's the drink of Proserpine
   On the bottom line.

Some day, when I am old and gray,
Perhaps retired (and rich), I'll pray
That bottom lines will fade away.
   No bottom lines.

With love and fear, O Bottom Line,
I worship you at Mammon's shrine.
I just can't get you off my mind.
   O Bottom Line.

Ah, but the bottom line is not enough; in addition to the profit-and-loss statement there must be a balance sheet and a cash flow analysis.

QUOTH THE BANKER, "WATCH CASH FLOW."

Once upon a midnight dreary as I pondered weak and weary
Over many a quaint and curious volume of accounting lore,
Seeking gimmicks (without scruple) to squeeze through some
   new tax loophole,
Suddenly I heard a knock upon my door.
      Only this, and nothing more.

Then I felt a queasy tingling and I heard the cash a-jingling
As a fearsome banker entered that I'd often seen before.
His face was money-green and in his eyes there could be seen
Dollar-signs that seemed to glitter as he reckoned up the score.
    "Cash flow," the banker said, and nothing more.

I had always thought it fine to show a jet black bottom line,
But the banker sounded a resounding, "No,
Your receivables are high, mounting upward toward the sky;
Write-offs loom. What matters is cash flow."
    He repeated, "Watch cash flow."

Then I tried to tell the story of our lovely inventory
Which, though large, is full of most delightful stuff.
But the banker saw its growth, and with a mighty oath
He waved his arms and shouted, "Stop! Enough!
    Pay the interest, and don't give me any guff!"

Next I looked for non-cash items which could add ad infinitum
To replace the ever-outward flow of cash,
But to keep my statement black I'd held depreciation back,
And my banker said that I'd done something rash.
    He quivered, and his teeth began to gnash.

When I asked him for a loan, he responded, with a groan,
That the interest rate would be just prime plus eight,
And to guarantee my purity he'd insist on some security—
All my assets plus the scalp upon my pate.
    Only this, a standard rate.

Though my bottom line is black, I am flat upon my back.
My cash flows out and customers pay slow.
The growth of my receivables is almost unbelievable;
The result is certain—unremitting woe!

And I hear the banker utter an ominous low mutter,
"Watch cash flow."

I have never been able to compose a satisfactory dirge on the balance sheet. Publishers must study balance sheets and be able to tell good ones from bad, even though the damn things always balance.

In closing I want to call the attention of readers to the Epilogue. A publishing friend gave me his opinion that it is the most important statement in the book, and I think he is right. I wish for all readers the greatest success in publishing, and as much enjoyment and satisfaction as I have had in my forty years as an editor and publisher.

Herbert S. Bailey, Jr.

May 1, 1990

THE ART AND SCIENCE OF BOOK PUBLISHING

I

IRRATIONALITY AND RATIONALITY IN PUBLISHING

THIS BOOK IS ABOUT BOOK PUBLISHING, which is quite different from magazine or newspaper publishing. To the usual definition of "to publish," namely "to make public," we add "in the form of a book." For convenience and brevity we will refer to book publishing simply as "publishing." Of course there are many ways of making things public, including radio and television broadcasting and shouting from rooftops, but book publishing is an identifiable separate activity with its own special social and cultural importance. It would be superfluous here to define "a book" or to elaborate on the place of the book in history and in the modern world. It is perhaps worth noting that a book, with its length, cheapness, portability, re-readability, and general convenience, provides opportunities for communication of expression and for the dissemination of ideas and information far different from those afforded by any other medium.

In the following pages I will attempt to present a descriptive and to some extent prescriptive, pragmatic view of management in book publishing. The book takes ideas from the fields of "management science" and financial management; it assumes that the manager of a publishing house is a rational man working with rational people in a rational environment, seeking objectives which may be complex but are at least defined and which are often expressed in monetary or at least numerical terms. During the writing of these chapters, which indeed have their own interest and excitement for me and, I hope, for others, I was troubled by the feeling that I had been leaving something out—that somehow the written words did not convey the swirl and excitement that permeates all aspects of publishing, including management. Leafing through an issue of the *Publishers' Weekly*, looking at the articles but especially at the advertisements for new books, I was struck by the thought that *this*, the brashness, the sensationalism, the exaggeration, the emotion and irrationality, was publishing, not the orderly image that I had been trying to present.

Of course, this is a true picture, and management must take the irrationality of publishing into account, not try to contain it within an orderly framework but live and work with it, internally and externally, participating in it and trying to comprehend and even anticipate it, encouraging it, criticizing it, relating it to the orderly aspects of the publishing house that are necessary for the existence and functioning of publishing.

It has been said that the three distinguishing characteristics of the modern world are the harnessing of power other than animal power, the universal application of reason, and the consciousness of the power of irrationality. Publishing uses the power of modern machines to produce and disseminate its productions, it applies rationality to its own organization and functioning, and it is immersed in a sea of irrationality to which it responds and which it stimulates. Much of the creativity that feeds publishing grows out of irrationality, the workings of the subconscious thoughts and desires of authors; and the multitudes of readers, whom we have been calling the market, are also moved by their own individual subconscious thoughts and desires. If a publishing house is a matching device, which we shall discuss in Chapter II, then it is often matching the irrationality of readers to the irrationality of authors—and vice versa. This is especially true in the fields of fiction and poetry, but it is also true in nonfiction. The kinds of appeals that advertising makes, even to the readers of the *Publishers' Weekly*, who could be expected to be cool and businesslike about books, reveal a large irrational psychological component. The milieu in which the publishing house exists is dominated by the personalities of authors and the projections of those personalities on readers—or by the minds of authors, with all the idiosyncrasies of style that express the rationalities and irrationalities of those minds, and the influences of those minds on readers.

Style, after all, is an expression of personality—I mean style of thought, which includes literary style—and the difficulty of explaining or even defining style reveals its irrational aspect. And of course each publishing house has a style: the style of its editors (again, not literary style but style of performance), the style of its designers, the style of its advertising and selling, the style of its dealings with printers and booksellers and other external agencies, and the style of its management, which becomes an internal style and affects all the other manifestations of style. The personality of the publisher himself, his enthusiasms and moods and irrationalities as well as his rational decisions and carefully drawn policies, becomes an important influence on the publishing activity, as do the personalities of his principal assistants and managers. These irrational influences filter through the organization, affecting different staff members in different ways, depending on their own personalities and jobs.

In the larger publishing houses the influence of a single personality is usually more diffused, but it is always a factor, and a strong personality can set the style of a large establishment. Smaller houses often reflect strongly the personalities of one leader or a few leaders, and this is one of their great strengths, since it enables a house to deal with authors on a more personal basis. One of the problems of large houses, as we shall see in Chapter II, is to decentralize enough to enable departments to act independently and with their own personalities, without losing the economic advantages of large size. Giant publishing firms like Simon & Schuster and McGraw-Hill consist of many divisions, each of which is in fact a publishing house in its own field (adult trade, juvenile, etc.) with overall services such as order processing and warehousing supplied and with a comprehensive financial and administrative management. The general management in such companies must exercise central direction and control without smothering the stylistic idiosyncrasies of the subdivisions, so as to let the personalities of editors and managers be expressed in publishing programs. Such management calls for more than the usual amount of administrative delicacy and sensitivity and understanding of personalities, to permit the development of imaginative initiative and flair and even irrational hunches, at the same time giving direction through rational analysis of internal and external operations.

In short, a publishing house is not a book-producing machine, an assembly of parts each with its unique and specific function; it is an organized group of human beings, each with his own rational and irrational characteristics, engaged in an activity that influences and reflects society with all its rationalities and irrationalities, its enthusiasms and problems and desires and fads and institutions and purposes. A publishing house is permeated with the interest and variety and excitement of the books it publishes. The management of this activity shares its rational and its irrational aspects, and although this book concentrates on the rational aspects, it should be kept in mind that both aspects are essential and that it is in the successful combination of both that the manager in publishing finds his satisfaction.

As the title indicates, the real subject of this book is the art and science of publishing management—the job of the publisher as the manager of a publishing house. The discussion necessarily involves other jobs, the jobs of the various departments and the relations among them, and it deals with the economics of the publishing house both in general and in detail. It examines the flows of work and the sequences of decisions that must be made at various levels and at various times, and it looks at the factors that go into those decisions and the policies that may govern them. There is probably not much, if anything, in the book that will be new to an experienced publisher, though its analytical and functional approach may present familiar things to him in a new light and stimulate a reexamination of his own practices.

Other members of publishing houses—editors, designers, production men, marketing experts, accountants—may find that the book helps them to see their own jobs more clearly in relation to the other departments and to the house as a whole; in fact this is one of the principal aims of the book. I hope that booksellers, librarians, authors, and others outside but close to the publishing industry will also find it interesting and helpful.

I do not know of any other book on publishing management, though there are many good books on publishing. The best general introduction is *What Happens in Book Publishing*, edited by Chandler B. Grannis, and another "required text" for a publisher is *The Truth About Publishing* by Stanley Unwin. Neither of these books overlaps this one to any significant degree. There are also many fine books on the literary side of publishing—one of the best is Maxwell Perkins' letters, *Editor to Author*—but this book hardly touches that fascinating and important area. Nor does it go into detail on the technical aspects of editing, designing, printing, marketing, or accounting; other books have dealt with those subjects excellently (see the reading list at the end of this book). It may be objected that what makes a great publishing house are great books, written by great authors, edited by great editors, designed with taste, produced with skill and efficiency, and energetically and widely sold. This is all true, but the subject here is not how to do all these essential things, but how these activities may be organized and coordinated and financed.

In Chapter II, "The External and Internal Environments of Publishing," we first look at the publishing house in relation to authors and readers, with some elaboration and refinement. We next turn to the internal structure, work flow, and communication within a publishing house, and we develop a schematic diagram indicating relationships. We then consider the question of personnel with an eye to selection, training, and advancement.

Chapter III, "Flows, Sequences, and Decisions," deals mainly with the activity of a publishing house over time. After introducing the terms "macro-publishing" and "micro-publishing," the chapter concentrates on macro-publishing, the operation of the publishing house as a whole, with its various flows of work and money and its sequences of decisions, including a discussion of the balance sheet and operating statement.

Chapter IV, "The Economics of Micro-Publishing," examines and analyzes the decisions that must be made with respect to an individual book, especially the determination of the price, the number to print in the first printing, and the question of reprinting. Some elementary algebra is used, and graphic representation is emphasized in order to show the relationships of the variables on which the publisher must exercise his judgment.

Chapter V, on "Planning," deals with that often neglected but important subject, considering briefly not only financial plans but other objectives in relation to the book market and changing technologies. This discussion leads directly to Chapter VI, "The New Technologies."

Some readers will probably find this book difficult because it works at two different levels. Chapters I, II, V, and VI should be easily comprehensible to beginners in publishing; Chapters III and IV are more technical and will be more difficult for beginners, though I hope worth the effort. These two chapters, I think, have most to say to responsible managers and officers who must cope daily with the problems discussed.

There is also a certain amount of necessary repetition because, in its emphasis on the working of a publishing house as a whole, the book cuts across traditional departmental lines. Thus the various departments—editorial, design, production, and accounting—

are treated in different contexts, resulting in a certain amount of overlapping, especially between Chapters II and III.

In Chapters III and IV some elementary economic theory will be used in the discussion of the problems of determining pricing and print orders and the like. In these discussions the classical concept of the economic man will be assumed—the man who desires to maximize profits or minimize losses regardless of other considerations—since this concept makes it possible to bring out relationships most clearly. But assuming this does not mean that the publisher will or should act in this way, though the pressures to do so may be strong. In fact few if any publishers really do behave like the classical economic man, though when talking to boards of directors or stockholders they might seem to do so.

Book publishers, even if they should want to, cannot escape from the role that books play in society, or from the image that they have of themselves as publishers and as citizens, or from the expectations of others who look upon them as participants in a long and honorable tradition. Nor can the manager of a publishing house escape from the self-images and aspirations of his subordinates, even if he should be completely cynical. Effective editors in any field of publishing must care about style and content, and if they do, they will not be satisfied to work with profit as the only measure of their ability. Book salesmen must care about books—if they didn't, they would be selling something else more profitable—and no good salesman is content to see the books he sells merely as a commodity of negative or even neutral value.

It is true that in the annual output of publishing houses, there is a lot of trash, even some books that are morally reprehensible by most standards, though sometimes their publishers defend them. But the fact that they are defended indicates that the publisher either can justify publication by his own standards or feels the need to justify what he does by standards acceptable to society. There is a market for trash or for obscenity, however one defines those terms, and there are publishers who will supply that market. Different publishers have different standards, and a few have pretty low standards and are willing to publish just about anything that will sell at a profit, but most publishers are keenly conscious of their cultural role and are anxious to meet high standards whatever their field of publishing—fiction, poetry, criticism, educational, juvenile, scholarly, reference, et cetera. Most of them must also make a profit.

Of course there is nothing wrong with making a profit. Potential profit provides a motive for investment by people with no particular interest in books, and naturally the publisher and his staff are interested in their own incomes, which are often tied to profits. Profits provide the funds for expansion, and they also provide the freedom to risk projects that are worthwhile but may be unprofitable. The best-established firms with the most substantial profits are often the very ones that are most willing to publish poetry or scholarly works that are almost certain to mean financial loss. There are also nonprofit firms, such as some religious publishers and university presses; these are given the privilege of exemption from federal taxes because they exist not for the purpose of making a profit but primarily for some other socially desirable purpose. But since taxes are paid only on profits, the fact that nonprofit publishers are exempt indicates that they may make profits within reason, for purposes of expansion, for example, so long as they do not pay dividends or in other ways transfer the profits to individuals, and so long as they devote themselves to their chartered purpose. Most if not all nonprofit publishers are subsidized in some way, and the greatest advantage of tax exemption is their privilege of receiving tax-exempt contributions from individuals, corporations, or foundations.

Whether a publisher is profit-oriented or nonprofit, he must carry out the various functions of publishing that are discussed in this book. The problem of maximizing profit is essentially the same as the problem of minimizing loss, and profit or nonprofit publishing is a matter of objectives, not of modes of operation.

And as we have seen, even objectives are a matter of degree and emphasis. The textbook publisher wants to publish books that will improve teaching and thereby enable him to make a profit; the university press publisher wants to publish important books of scholarly research and minimize publishing losses. It is not surprising that people move easily back and forth between profit and nonprofit publishing, adapting themselves to the objectives of the firm they work in and utilizing the same knowledge and skills.

A publishing house exists for objectives that are officially determined by the board of directors and top management, in varying degrees responsive to stockholders, but a firm's objectives also contain an ingredient of the objectives of its employees, who may care very much or not at all *what* the firm publishes or *how* it publishes but for whom work in the firm is an important part of life. This should be and usually is recognized, though often not explicitly. Or it takes various forms of expression such as "company loyalty," "employee morale," or "loyalty up and loyalty down." The firm exists not only for its stated primary objectives (dividends to stockholders, publication of valuable books) but for the people in it, enabling them so far as possible to live fruitful and satisfying lives, rewarding them for their efforts not only in salaries but in satisfaction and security. A wise publisher will understand this and respect his employees entirely aside from the need to retain them in the face of competition for personnel, though this may be an important motivation. He will pay attention to the aspirations of his colleagues, will make compromises or even sometimes go against his own judgment, will provide rewards in recognition and honor as well as in salary.

The wise publisher will not replace an employee of long service who through illness or age may be not so effective as a younger man might be, though he may have to reorganize his area of work in order to meet operational needs. Sometimes an organization changes or grows rapidly in ways that are difficult or impossible for some employees to adapt to, and if this happens, the publisher will need to use imagination and ingenuity to avoid being harsh or unfair to loyal workers. People have different abilities and capacities, and the catch phrase "Use a man for what he's good for" has its positive as well as its negative aspects. People are happier and more effective if they are given jobs that utilize their abilities well. This is why publishing houses, when viewed in detail, are organized in so many different ways.

The management, accounting, editorial, design, production, and marketing functions must be performed, but the patterns and arrangements of responsibilities may be infinitely varied to utilize the abilities and meet the desires of the particular people doing the work. In the following chapters much will be said about these functions and activities, but nothing is intended to mean that a rigid structure is desirable; the structure must be flexible enough to change when the people change. If it does not and if the firm is not able to satisfy in sufficient degree the objectives of the people who work in it, it will not be able to satisfy its own objectives.

Thus it is clear that neither the publishing house as a whole nor its employees individually can be expected to behave like the classical economic man, motivated only by considerations of profit or loss. Let us keep this in mind as we proceed to discuss and analyze various aspects of publishing operations. For analytical purposes it may be said that the publisher "should" do so-and-so, but such statements must be read in context. No amount of analysis will take the judgment out of publishing, but analysis can help a publisher make better judgments in the pursuit of his objectives, providing a clear background of relationships against which judgments may be made.

II

THE EXTERNAL AND INTERNAL ENVIRONMENTS OF PUBLISHING

In its largest sense, the environment of publishing is the world, and because books can deal with every possible subject, publishing touches every aspect of knowledge. The function of publishing is to supply books to the world. This very broad conception of the external environment of publishing is not very useful, however, and a simpler and more functional view shows the publishing house with authors on one side and readers on the other. The publishing house is a matching device between the author and the reader. The publisher seeks and is sought by authors, he selects manuscripts and transforms them into books, and he seeks or is sought by readers. His problem is to match the readers to the authors, or at least to the particular books. At the same time, of course, he is matching the authors to the readers. Schematically, it can be seen (Figure 1) that the publisher looks two ways and that he serves a social and cultural function by performing this matching. This is true whether the books are fiction or nonfiction, adult or juvenile, educational or recreational, and so forth. In an electrical analogy, the publisher is a filter, transformer, and transmitter between senders and receivers.

The analogy seems obvious, but this essential relationship is sometimes ignored within publishing houses, where a designer may be intent upon making an especially beautiful book or a production man may be interested in the efficient use of particular equipment, without reference to the external aspects. The publisher, as manager, must supply sensitivity where it is lacking; he must constantly look both ways at once, and of course we have presented a much oversimplified picture of the external environment. On the authors' side it is very diverse. There are established authors with whom the house has continuous working relationships, there are occasional authors and loners, there are institutional authors and authors within institutions, and there are literary agents who stand between the author and the publisher, each representing a number of authors and acting as a preliminary filter.

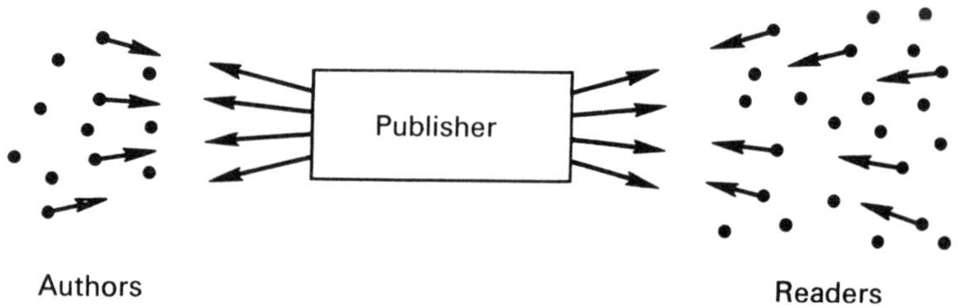

Figure 1

The environment of a publishing house also includes other publishing houses which are competing for the same authors, institutional or otherwise. House authors are wooed away. Institutional authors are approached or seek other arrangements. Literary agents are notoriously ready to switch an author from one publisher to another, and they are constantly in touch with many publishers. The loners can choose among many publishers. The activities and decisions of a publishing house are profoundly influenced by the constellation of authors that it sees as sources and by the competition it experiences from other publishers.

Looking in the direction of readers, the publisher sees an even more complicated situation. In the first place, the market for books in English is worldwide; anyone who can read English is a potential reader. But except for certain kinds of books, the emphasis will be on the domestic market. Here the publisher faces a curious problem; he must seek the readers, but they do not directly seek him. For any individual book the publisher will

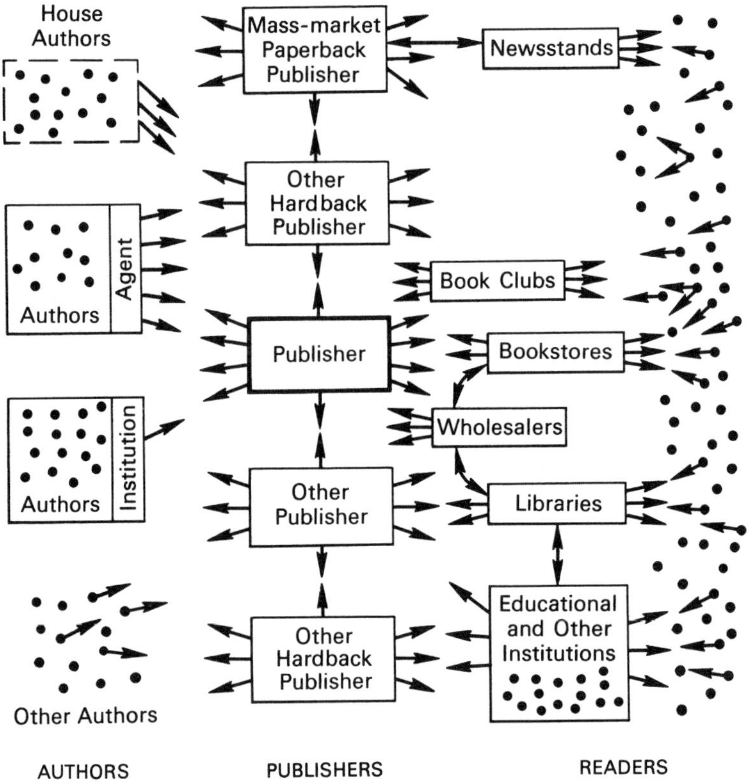

Figure 2

imagine a number of readerships, individuals interested in a certain subject or a certain kind of fiction, for example, or institutional readers such as schoolchildren. He will publicize his book in various ways, hoping to interest these readers, but those who want the book will seek it indirectly through bookstores or libraries or wholesalers. Thus the marketing activity must be very flexible and varied, alert to the interests of many groups in many locations, aware of changing patterns of communication to a variety of publics. This is indicated schematically in Figure 2.

Thus the publishing house is Janus-faced, looking two ways. Or, to change the image, the publisher simultaneously juggles authors with his right hand and readers with his left, and this requires a high degree of coordination. This coordination must be achieved by a flow of information through the mind of the juggler—or the minds of the publisher and his colleagues in the publishing house. Later we will consider this internal flow, but the important point here is that the flow must exist in any publishing house. The editorial side, which deals with authors, must be aware of the activities and problems of the marketing side, which deals directly or indirectly with readers—and vice versa.

Complexity can be managed either by more complexity or by specialization, and the complexity of the situation shown in Figure 2 has led to both solutions. The most obvious one is specialization, and there are many kinds of specialty publishers: educational or text, technical, adult trade, reference, religious, juvenile, university presses, book clubs, "quality" paperback, mass market paperback, and so forth. Each has its special relationships with authors and readers. There are also large publishing houses embracing many or all of these fields, but to work effectively, such houses are always organized in semi-independent divisions, each like a smaller specialized publishing house. In large houses, however, certain activities, especially financial and managerial, are centralized, which is necessary in maintaining coordination between the right hand and the left hand, though it also can lead to difficulties.

The existence of these many specialties in publishing makes it apparent that all publishing is part of something else. The educational houses are part of the educational system; the religious publishing houses are part of organized religion; university presses are part of the activity of scholarly research in universities; technical publishers are part of the scientific establishment; and so forth. Each of these specialties can be seen, and each must see itself, in relation to the larger structure of which it is a part. Indeed this function within the larger structure is forcibly brought to bear in various ways; if the function is not served, the house fails or is reorganized. Many religious publishing houses are controlled by religious organizations, directly or indirectly, and serve to propagate the ideas of a particular denomination or sect. All university presses are controlled in significant degree by faculty committees and are ultimately responsible to university authorities. Educational publishers, above all, must meet the needs of schools and colleges or fail.

These relationships do not necessarily mean that publishers are mere tools, helpless cogs in the larger machinery; it means that the publisher works within a particular environment that is not publishing, responding to it and influencing its development in varying degree. A strong and creative publishing house can have important long-term effects by encouraging certain authors and certain areas of writing and certain ideas, by finding readers for those authors and gaining acceptance for those ideas. A strong house can experiment and innovate, it can afford occasional failures, it can persist in propagating unpopular ideas or points of view, but it can do these things effectively only if it maintains its basic function within the larger activity of which it is a part. This does not necessarily mean that it must always sell enough books to be financially self-supporting as a whole, despite some money-losing activities. The larger structure—for example, a church or university—may consider the publishing function important enough to justify financial support. There are even cases in which a publishing house, by trying to become self-supporting, failed to perform its function within its larger structure and had to be reorganized; this could happen to a university press, for example.

We have been examining publishing as a matching process, authors on one side and readers on the other, and there must be communication both ways: the authors' manuscripts are or are not accepted by the publishing house; the readers buy or do not buy the books. Figure 1 shows the readers as being different from the authors, but in many fields of publishing, especially the specialized and professional fields, this is not so. The readers to a large extent *are* the authors or are professionally *like* the authors. Every author is also a reader. In such fields the feedback from readers to authors is very powerful and very direct. The author responds to criticism from his professional colleagues, especially as expressed in reviews. The publisher will usually seek professional opinions of a manuscript in a special or professional field before agreeing to publish, and the author will take advantage of such criticisms in revising the manuscript. Thus the publisher acts not only as a matching device but also as a means of maintaining and improving professional standards in the field. In such circumstances the publisher builds a reputation within a field, developing relationships with leading professionals and achieving recognition as a source of important books. In this situation there is a snowball effect, and success leads to success because of the large degree of direct feedback. For the same reasons, failures can be very important; publishing a bad book or developing bad relations with a leading author can have severe and ramifying repercussions.

This discussion will seem strange to those who think of publishing as identical with "adult trade," or "general," publishing. General publishing, which is not specialized by definition, is the most visible part of publishing because it appeals to the "general public"—or more properly the "general reading public," which is a small percentage of the general public, sad to say. General publishers publish nearly all of the current fiction and popular nonfiction, the books that are reviewed in the Sunday book review and are displayed in bookstore windows. Large advertising campaigns are mounted, television and movie rights are sold, rights are sold to book clubs for their monthly distribution. In other words, these are nonspecialist books and must be promoted and sold to the small proportion of "general readers" that are mingled in the general public. These readers must be reached through general advertising, visible to everybody, though it is usually assumed that they, because they are readers, will scan book review sections or look at bookstore windows. Adult trade publishers are specialists at reaching the nonspecialist reading public. It is the riskiest branch of publishing; the publisher bets on his judgment of popular taste, which is notoriously unpredictable.

Actually, of course, there is no such thing as a "general" book, any more than there is a "general reader." Every book can be classified in some way: detective story, science fiction, literary novel, poetry, popular science, self-help, historical, religious, and so forth. The author wrote the book with some readership, perhaps vaguely conceived, in mind, and the publisher believes he can find readers for the book. Some readership groups can be identified and located, even for adult trade books, but the prime characteristic of adult trade publishing is that the readership is varied and amorphous, difficult and expensive to reach, with tastes that can be described generally but that are hard to match to a specific book. Failures in this field are frequent but the rewards of success are great. Thus in adult trade publishing there is an enormous amount of competitive energy expended in the other direction, that is, in the direction of authors, especially those with an established reputation and an eager following of readers. The agents of such authors drive hard bargains in guaranteed advance royalties, high royalty rates, shares of subsidiary rights, and so forth.

Mention of money leads us to another aspect of the publishing environment, an aspect that must always be a part of a publisher's total perception. Publishing is an activity—a cultural and social activity, but also a business activity. Investment capital is necessary, books must be sold and money collected, and the printer's bill must be paid. Money flows from the customers (readers) to bookstores and wholesalers and then to publishers, and from the publishers it flows to authors, printers, advertising media, stockholders, and so forth. As money flows through these stages, portions are diverted to pay for the activity at each stage, including the profit that is necessary for virtually all private businesses. Thus the publisher works in a business environment that includes stockholders, banks, creditors, customers, and sometimes associates in other activities where subsidiary rights may be sold (book clubs, television) or where books may be created (educational institutions, government agencies) or where production processes may be affected (printers, electronics industry) or where basic rights may be affected (lawyers, government), and so forth. He thinks in terms of contracts, discounts, royalties, manufacturing costs, publishing expenses, taxes, budgets, and profit or loss.

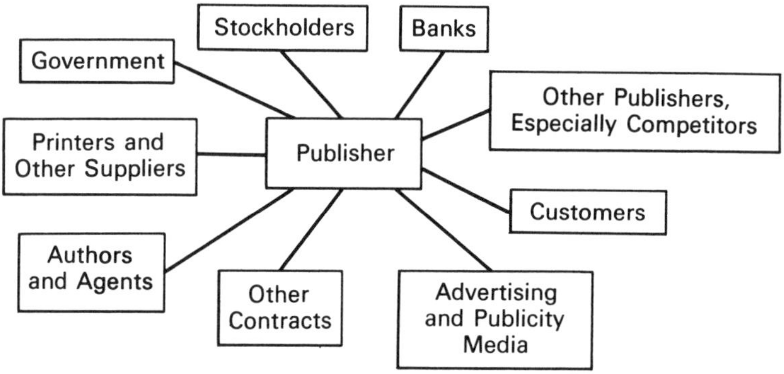

Figure 3

Figure 3 suggests the business environment, which we shall discuss in more detail later. The point here is that the social and cultural publishing activity, selecting manuscripts from authors and transforming and distributing them as books, is conducted as a complex business activity in which the bills must be paid, the books must be sold, the budget must balance, and a profit must be provided.

The business environment of publishing provides both a large degree of freedom and a certain stringency. In America almost anything can be published. Although there are always groups who would like to censor or suppress certain publications, the First Amendment to the Constitution is a bastion of defense. Publishers and other groups concerned with freedom of expression and freedom of information constantly skirmish with censorship groups. Censorship laws are frequently proposed locally and in state legislatures and in Congress; they are opposed but occasionally are passed, and then they must be fought in the courts. The price of freedom is vigilance, and publishers have on the whole been vigilant in protecting the right to publish, both individually and through their associations. The entrepreneurial character of publishing helps to insure this vigilance, since a publication that appeals to minority opinion may still be financially profitable.

Moreover, in American society there are many individuals and institutions (foundations, universities, churches, corporations) that will support publication of unpopular ideas, supplying funds to reimburse a publisher for a loss or even to pay outright to have certain material published. It is possible in America to publish works advocating unorthodox religious ideas or even the radical transformation of society; the chief areas of significant proscription are libel and obscenity, and even here the laws are very permissive. Libel applies only to the living, and truth is usually sufficient as a defense. Public figures are protected only minimally against libel, although recently privacy in personal matters has been increasingly recognized as a right. As for obscenity, a quick look at what is being published will convince anyone that the limits are very far out; only the most "hard core" pornography is illegal, and legislators find it difficult if not impossible to frame laws to proscribe that without invading areas of legitimate publication.

The entrepreneurial character of publishing also insures a certain stringency, even with publications receiving outside support. Profit-oriented publishers want to maximize profits and tend to avoid books that are expected to lose money. Nonprofit and mission-oriented publishers must justify their losses to the suppliers of funds. Thus the environment tends to insure a stringency that leads to efficiency, while at the same time providing an openness that is conducive to variety and freedom.

Publishing is responsive to the general social environment, which can in turn be influenced by it. This is seen especially clearly in educational publishing—since education in America is preponderantly public, since it reflects the ideals and aspirations of society, since it is mainly controlled by a government (at every level) which responds to society, and since it is the largest single market for books. Regional preferences (urban emphasis, treatment of Negroes) are reflected in schoolbooks, and at the same time publishers attempt to devise educational programs that will improve education and be attractive to specific educational groups. New educational materials developed and promoted by publishers, usually in collaboration with educators, affect trends in education. This is not to say that everything goes smoothly. Competition produces its casualties; publishing houses fail or are merged. Powerful groups of educators, government agencies, university researchers, or school boards exert their influence. In education the various branches and levels of government play especially important roles. The alert publisher observes and maintains relations with the various factions, and by free interaction with a social, cultural, and financial environment the publisher influences and is influenced.

The result of all this effort is an enormous amount of publishing, including much that is worthless and some that even liberally inclined readers might consider positively harmful, but including also a remarkable richness and variety of great social and cultural value. The waste of the worthless or harmful publications is the price of the freedom that permits uninhibited variety, innovation, and originality—in contrast to the products of publishing in countries that cannot afford waste or that must control publication for political reasons. Publishers in Yugoslavia, for example, where they have more independence than in most communist countries, must submit detailed plans for approval by a central committee a year in advance. In some countries the allocation of paper and printing facilities by a government agency is a means of controlling publication. Where publishing is controlled by government ministries, the selection of material to be published tends to fall into the hands of factions or doctrinaire groups, even where the intent is to permit freedom of expression and thought.

In the preceding section we have seen publishing in its external environment; we have been looking at the environment from the point of view of the publisher, outlining his relationships to authors, readers, other publishers, other parts of the publishing industry, and society in general. The publisher must be sensitive to this environment and live in it, and he can do this more successfully if he understands what he looks like to his environment—to authors, readers, and so forth.

The author, to begin with, probably does not know very much about publishing, even if he is an experienced author. Moreover he is not interested in publishing except as it applies to his own book, in which he is rightfully *very* interested. He has expended a large effort on it, and it is his brain child. He wants it to be read, and he wants monetary recompense for his effort. How will he seek or select a publisher?

If he is wise, he will first look at the books on his own shelf, the books that he uses and knows. Which books are most like his book, and who published them? Which publishers specialize in his field? Who publishes the most important and most respected books in his field? Can he make a list of publishers in order of preference?

This list may be modified after the author has examined the publishers' catalogues, read their advertisements, and considered the design and quality of printing of several publishers' books (he wants his brain child to be well-dressed!).

Many authors are advised by other authors and by agents who

have had experience with various publishers. Is publisher X fair and easy to deal with? Does he reach decisions quickly? How long will he take to get the book out? Will his editors do a good job without mutilating the book? Will he do a good job of advertising and selling?

The wise author will send a description of his book to a publisher before sending the manuscript itself. If possible he will discuss the manuscript with an editor. Then, if the publishing house encourages him, he will submit the manuscript (or outline or partial manuscript) and wait. He must be prepared for rejection and must have the courage to continue to submit to other publishers until his manuscript is accepted. He must also be willing to revise or at least to consider revision in the light of criticism that he may receive from the publisher. In all, submitting a manuscript is a trying experience, and one cannot blame authors for being somewhat edgy or for feeling that publishers are "the enemy," standing between authors and their readers. On the other hand, especially when the publisher is sensitive to the author's feelings, it is possible to have a very warm and mutually satisfying and helpful relationship. In this circumstance the author must understand and trust the publisher's judgment too, but inevitably the author's emotions are more deeply involved than the publisher's.

Occasionally an impatient author will submit several copies of his manuscript to several publishers. This is understandable and is really not objectionable *so long as each publisher is told that the manuscript is also being considered elsewhere.* The publisher has a right to expect full and honest information from an author, just as the author expects honest treatment from the publisher. Since consideration of manuscripts is time-consuming and expensive, a publisher's attitude toward a manuscript may be affected if he knows it has been simultaneously offered to other publishers; he may compete harder for it or may pass it by quickly, preferring not to risk the effort of detailed consideration.

Many established authors prefer to stay with a single publisher who has done well with their previous work and whose editors they know and respect. Also, a publisher who has helped to build the reputation of an author can expect some loyalty (which must be mutual!), though in today's increasingly competitive publishing such loyalty is beginning to be exceptional. But loyalty aside, there are often real advantages to both author and publisher in a continuing relationship, as each book helps to build the reputation and readership and sales of earlier books, just as the earlier books have built a readership for that author's writing.

What has just been said about authors can also be said about agents, but it should not need to be said to them since they are supposed to be experts at placing manuscripts with publishers—and at getting the best terms from publishers. No publisher should object to dealing with an agent, so long as the agent really knows his business and has the author's best long-term interests in mind. Unfortunately there are incompetent and short-sighted agents, just as there are incompetent and short-sighted authors and publishers, but many agents are exceedingly helpful to authors. In business matters some publishers prefer to deal with agents rather than authors, since an agent's emotions are less involved and he usually has a more realistic and experienced judgment of a manuscript's publishing potential. But in editorial matters there is no substitute for direct communication between the author and the editor; the editor's and the author's interests coincide, and the editor's reactions to a manuscript and his suggestions for revisions can be invaluable to the author.

The reader's view of a publisher is much more remote, and few readers even know the names of publishing houses. Their source of books is the bookstore or the library. They browse and pick up books that interest them, or they ask for a particular book by a particular author, paying no attention whatever to the name of the publisher. Publishers, through their advertising, try to impress on readers the importance of the imprint as a reliable source of good books, but to a large degree this effort is fruitless. The chief exceptions are in specialized areas, especially in professional fields such as medicine or science, where a large number of readers are potential or aspiring authors and where a publisher may build a reputation as a source of important books in a particular field. But even though a publisher's imprint may mean little or nothing to readers, it may be effective in getting books to those same readers because bookstores and libraries are quite aware of differences among publishers, and their efforts to make a book known and available may be conditioned by their confidence in the publisher.

We have been examining the external environment of publishing, especially the publishers' relations to authors and readers. We have seen that these relations are structured by the publisher's social and cultural functions and by financial considerations. We shall now turn to the internal aspects of publishing, as the publisher strives to carry out his functions in this external environment.

INSIDE A PUBLISHING HOUSE

In organizing to perform their function in relation to the external environment, publishing houses have developed various standard departments, each of which is a subactivity. There are a number of slight variations in the arrangement of these departments, but the functions they carry out must be performed somehow in order to transform the manuscripts of authors into books for readers.

The usual departments of a publishing house are:

Editorial
Design
Production
Marketing
Accounting
Management.

It will immediately be seen that the last two departments are quite different in nature from the first four. There is a natural flow from the author to the editorial department, where the manuscript is selected and edited, to the design department, where its physical form is specified, to the production department, where books are actually produced (or production with an outside printer is supervised), and to the marketing department, where the books are sold directly or indirectly to readers. We shall examine this flow and these subactivities in more detail, but first it should be noted that accounting and management involve all of them. The accounting department keeps detailed records of income and expense, providing management with background information and future projections on the basis of which man-

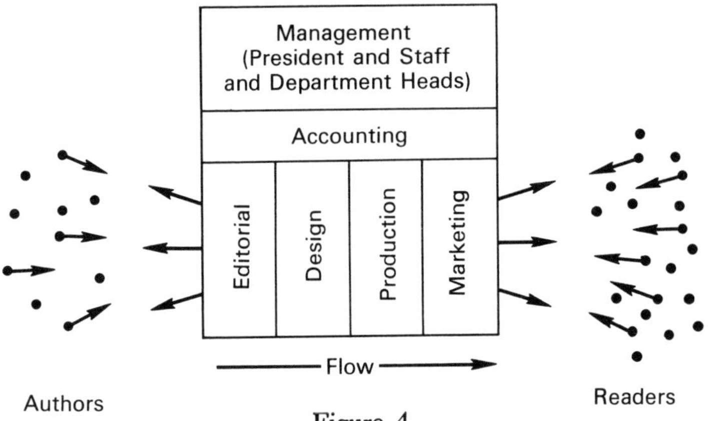

Figure 4

agement can make decisions. The accounting department also processes orders, collects bills, and controls credit, and shipping and warehousing are often responsibilities of the accounting department. Management does not ordinarily consider itself a department, since it controls all the others; it usually consists of the publisher (the president with his staff) and the heads of the various departments. The job of management is to control the overall activity of the publishing house both internally and with respect to its external environment. The management sets directions, goals, and policies, and it concerns itself with internal coordination. Thus Figure 1 might be modified as shown in Figure 4.

It is evident that the editorial department has direct contact with one part of the external environment and the marketing department with another. This of course affects the point of view of each, just as the design department is affected by its contact with editorial and production, and the production department is affected by design and marketing. Revealing as it is, even this diagram is oversimplified, for there is and must be a flow of information and influence all the way through the publishing house, in both directions, from editorial through to marketing and from marketing through to editorial. Each department has its needs and problems that affect all the others.

The Editorial Department

The editorial department, in its constant dealings with authors, represents the whole publishing house to the author. The author is interested in what will happen to his book, but in fact he is only minimally interested in what will happen to it editorially, except that he usually and understandably hopes for a minimum of editing beyond a helpful clean-up of punctuation, spelling, and internal consistency. The author is much more interested, after a manuscript has been accepted, in what his book will look like, how quickly it will be produced, what advertising and sales effort will be made, and what payment he will receive. But first the acceptability of the manuscript must be determined, and this is the prime responsibility of the editorial department.

Editors read manuscripts and write reports on them, recommending acceptance, revision, or rejection. These are internal reports for the purpose of making decisions; the publisher has no obligation to share them with the author, though he may wish to do so. Hundreds and often thousands of manuscripts come in to a publishing house each year, and every one must be dealt with by the editorial department. Many are quickly examined and immediately rejected; a few are as quickly and easily accepted, especially manuscripts from previously published authors whose work is known and valued. Still others are pondered over, read by various people, and accepted or rejected only after a careful and agonizing process; sometimes acceptance is conditional upon successful completion of certain revisions, or an author may be encouraged to revise and resubmit, with no guarantee of acceptance. Especially difficult is the proposal from an outline or on the basis of a partially completed manuscript. If the proposal is attractive the editor may be hesitant not to accept for fear that he will lose it to another publisher, but if he accepts he may be stuck with a worthless or unattractive manuscript.

Acceptance or rejection of proposals is a matter for judgment of possibilities and risks, and the judgment may extend to estimating a reasonable and safe guaranteed advance royalty payment and other contractual arrangements. A great deal of publishing is done on an advance-contract basis, especially with established authors or with specialists who may be counted on to write authoritatively about their specialty. Such advance contracts almost always contain escape clauses, permitting the publisher to back out if the finished manuscript is unsatisfactory, but publishers are extremely reluctant to do so since this would affect the publisher's reputation and the credibility of his other advance contracts.

Thus the judgment of the editorial department is applied not only to manuscripts submitted but to projects and ideas, and this judgment must grow out of a sense of the publishing house's overall purposes, goals, and abilities. If the house's main purpose is to produce a profit, and of course this is a primary consideration with most publishers, the editor must have some judgment of a project's sales and profit potential, but he must also judge the project on the basis of the house's own special interests and abilities. A technical publisher will usually not take on a cookbook even though it might be profitable; such a book would not fit into his program and would interfere with carrying out his major objectives; moreover it would not be consistent with the reputation he is trying to maintain with his reader-author public.

At the same time the editorial department is deciding which

manuscripts should be accepted, it is also seeking authors and trying to persuade them to accept the publisher. Editors are writing to potential authors and traveling to talk to authors and agents. They are reading newspapers and magazines and professional journals in their fields of interest, watching to see who is writing on what subjects and what ideas and subjects are currently in the public eye. They are talking to specialists of various kinds, getting recommendations of subjects and authors. They are thinking up projects and seeking authors to carry them out, and they are keeping in touch with authors whose work has been previously published by their house, inquiring what they will be writing next, encouraging, criticizing, and suggesting.

The editor who is persuading an author to bring his manuscript to his publishing house usually talks about everything *except* editing. From the author's point of view his manuscript, when it is finished, will say what he wants to say in the way he wants to say it, and it will not need editing. Actually, during the interview, some editing may be going on as the subject, emphasis, approach, organization, and possible readers are discussed, but this will not be thought of as editing. The editor's conversation will concern the physical form of the book, especially if illustrations are needed or if there are other special problems of format. He will talk about other related or similar books on his publishing house's list, what has been done to promote them, and the success they have had. He will discuss publishing schedules, and he will outline facilities and plans for publicity, advertising, and selling. He will discuss royalty arrangements, guarantees, ways of minimizing taxes, payment for required permissions, and other financial aspects. In short, he will represent the publisher to the author, and to do this well his knowledge of publishing generally and of his own house in particular must be substantial. The more he knows, and the more experience he has, the better he will be able to do his job.

In the course of his discussion, or in a series of discussions and correspondence, often in a semisocial atmosphere at lunch or over a drink, the editor will develop a personal relationship with the author. The author can benefit from a feeling of confidence that he is working with a sympathetic and understanding and helpful editor, and the publishing house can benefit from such a relationship with a productive and successful author. Nor should it be forgotten that the editor is not simply the creature of his publishing house. He is in publishing not just to earn a living, though that is essential, but because he is interested in books and ideas; and the satisfaction of working with authors to develop books that are worthwhile and successful, in whatever sense, is one of the rewards of his job.

The editor may become deeply involved in an author's project and may make important contributions to it; he can do this so long as he remembers that it is the author's book and not his own. Some editors go too far and invade the province of the author, and when this happens the editor is invariably met with hostility and withdrawal. Thus the editor must not only be conversant with the field in which he works and with the various aspects of publishing; he must also be sensitive to personal relationships, adaptable to various kinds of personalities and attitudes among authors, and always conscious of the limits as well as the possibilities of his role as editor.

The editor represents the publisher to the author, but he is *not* the publisher. After talking to the author, he must return to his office and represent the author to the publisher—in terms of the interests of the publisher. Usually the editor is not authorized to commit the publisher to the author except in a minimal way; the contract must be approved by the publisher. Even when the editor has authority to make substantial commitments, as some senior editors do, he is answerable to the publisher; he has such authority because his knowledge and experience are sufficient for him to anticipate the publisher's reactions and decisions. The publisher, after all, is not the editor, and he has the overall responsibility for the publishing program. The editor may become very involved in a project or with an author, and his involvement may cause him to lose perspective or lack judgment. He must usually, therefore, present his project (a complete or partial manuscript or a prospectus) to the publisher, who will consider it from a more general and objective point of view. The editor must present a budget for the project and estimate sales and income, perhaps consulting the marketing manager and examining sales records of similar books. Certainly he will get estimates of manufacturing cost from the production department. As a last step, he will consider the project in relation to the house's overall publishing program.

All this will be discussed between the editor and the publisher, and a publication plan in all its aspects will be evolved, at least in outline. If the editor's knowledge of publishing is sufficient, there should be no halt at this point, but if the publisher thinks the editor has misjudged the quality or appropriateness or financial prospects of the project, difficulties may ensue. Of course in a general sense the publisher must have confidence in the editor, and vice versa; without that they could not work together. But the editor may be relatively inexperienced or too much involved, or the publisher may have a different judgment or have problems the editor is not aware of. Then the publisher must exert his power of decision—to reject the project in spite of the editor's recommendation, to require the editor (and author) to modify the project in some way, or to back the editor and accept the project in spite of his own contrary judgment. The last course may be dictated by a desire to support the editor's overall program and to protect the editor's and the house's reputation and relationships with authors, particularly if the publisher has an awareness that his own judgment is fallible—and publishing is very conducive to that awareness! But whatever happens, the publisher must ultimately take the responsibility.

With the contract in his hand—or in some cases without a contract—the editor goes back to the author. There may be negotiation over terms with the author or his agent, and the publisher may have to be consulted again. Or the publisher himself may conduct such a negotiation after the project has been accepted in principle. If the editor must go back to the author without a contract, rejecting or asking for major revisions in a manuscript that he has encouraged, the situation can be very embarrassing. Such embarrassment is not really necessary, however; an experienced editor will rarely find himself in such a position, because he will make the complex relationships of author, editor, and publisher clear to the author. Although the editor represents the publisher to the author, he will emphasize that he himself is not the publisher and that what he and the author agree on must be approved by the publisher. The editor becomes the author's ally in developing a project that the publisher will approve, just as he is the publisher's ally in seeking authors and developing projects that will further the publisher's goals. He is not exactly in the middle, however; he is a part of the publishing house, and he is not likely to forget that he is on the publisher's payroll.

Let us suppose that the manuscript has been written and accepted, and the contract has been signed on terms that are agreeable to everyone. What happens next? Now the *real* editing must begin. The editor, who may have been involved with the manuscript from its origin as an idea in the author's mind, and who may even have suggested the idea, goes over the manuscript carefully for style and content. He tries to think of the book as a finished work making its way into the world, and he worries about everything from the title page to the colophon (if there is one). He considers the question of illustrations and diagrams: Are they good enough? Are they too expensive? Are permissions required? Are drawings needed? He examines the organization of the book and considers alternatives. He marks sections of the manuscript and makes notes that he will later share with the author. He tries to put himself in the place of the reader: What will the reader want to know? How will he approach the book? How can he be helped to get the most from it, in information and enjoyment?

The editor will then have a session or sessions with the author, perhaps leaving the manuscript for the author to revise in the light of his suggestions. The amount of substantive editing will vary greatly from book to book and among types of books. Manuscripts vary in their need of editing, and authors vary in their willingness to be edited.

When the substantive editing is completed, an editor, sometimes the same editor who has been following the project from the beginning but more often a specialist copyeditor, will go through the manuscript from beginning to end, at least two and often three or more times, scrutinizing every chapter and every paragraph and every sentence, checking consistency and spelling and punctuation, looking for ways to improve organization and phrasing, cutting out redundancies and asking for elaboration of points that are not clear, asking questions that a reader might ask but that had not occurred to the author. The copyeditor is probably not an expert on the subject of the manuscript, but he (or she; a high proportion of copyeditors are women) should be an intelligent and careful reader, an expert on the mechanics of writing and a connoisseur of style, a helpful and sensitive critic, and an interpreter of the author's wishes to the designer and the printer. Usually, if the copyeditor is a different person from the acquisitions editor (or list-building editor or procurement editor; there is no standard term), the two will work closely together on any problems that may arise. The copyeditor must exercise tact and judgment; he must get the job done properly without antagonizing the author, and this is not always easy. Some authors are glad to have all the help they can get, but others resent the changing of so much as a comma. Not one in a hundred manuscripts comes from the author ready for the printer, so some copyediting is always necessary. At the very least the copyeditor will see the manuscript through production, checking proofs and answering queries of the printer and of the author. The copyeditor's role is an exacting and often a thankless one, but a good copyeditor will occasionally win an author's undying gratitude, and unquestionably the copyeditor contributes enormously to the quality, soundness, and orderliness of the house's publications.

The copyeditor must be able to make himself interested in whatever he is working on. He may have to do some background reading, and he will certainly want to do a good deal of checking in reference works of various kinds. The copyeditor is himself a kind of walking Webster, with an admixture of Fowler, Strunk and White, Bernstein, and other pundits of style. From the experience of previous editing and from wide reading, the copyeditor brings to the manuscript a broad knowledge combined with a relentless inquisitiveness, plus patience and an ability to deal with detail. The copyeditor, pencil in hand, works on the manuscript preparing it for the printer, checking with the author as necessary. He visualizes the book as a finished work, printed and between covers, and he anticipates where the printer may go wrong. He also works closely with the designer, and in some houses a designer is assigned to a book at the same time as the copyeditor so that design questions can be settled as they come up. Then the designer will already be familiar with the book when it reaches the design department, and the work of design can proceed more quickly and smoothly.

The Design Department

Most readers, with their attention concentrated on the words of the author, do not think of books as being "designed," yet they will respond to the appeal of a beautifully designed book or will be grateful for ease and pleasure in reading a well-designed page. The designer specifies the physical form of the book—the type page and margins, the title page, the binding, and the jacket, often making drawings or selecting decorative material—and the world of books would be far less interesting and attractive if it were not for the great tradition of bookmaking and the innovations of modern designers.

Yet the design department is the problem department of many publishing houses, and in fact some publishers try to avoid problems by having no design department at all and relying on freelance designers. But someone must supervise the freelance designers, checking schedules and approving designs, so the problems may be there anyway. In fact many of the problems usually attributed to design departments are inherent and are not the fault of designers. Everyone thinks he is an expert on book design, and the author, editor, marketing manager, and production manager may all have different ideas about how any particular book should look.

Design is an art, and designers as artists tend to be individualistic, which may also trouble a publisher. In general, designers do not fall into administrative patterns easily. The better the design department, the more likely that the designers are individualistic, and the more it tends not to be an organized department at all but a collection of individual designers. The designer-artist relies on a certain degree of inspiration, which cannot be turned on at will. He must familiarize himself with a manuscript, mull over it, imagine various ways of treating it typographically, and then work out a design in detail. For inspiration he may visit art galleries, or he may dig in the library for appropriate visual material.

The designer may make false starts, or he may evolve a design that pleases him but that the author or the editor or the marketing manager or the publisher does not like. This situation, which leads to arguments and unsatisfactory compromises, can be avoided or minimized if the designer works closely with the editor and with the marketing department from the beginning. They should provide a preliminary conception of the physical form of the book before it has crystallized in the designer's mind. They will have suggestions that may stimulate the designer's imagination. The editor will also convey the author's preferences, and often it is helpful for the designer to talk to the author, though the author should not be permitted to specify the design since he cannot take full account of the various publishing considerations. The marketing department will have suggestions especially for the jacket, which plays an important advertising role. A certain visual emphasis may be desired, and the marketing department will be interested in how the jacket will look in displays in bookstores.

Most of all, however, the designer will need to communicate with the production department. What type fonts are available? How will the book be printed? What are the special production problems that must be anticipated by the designer? The relations between the design department and the production department are so close that often the design department is a part of the production department, responsible to the production manager. If the publisher is mainly interested in economy and is willing to publish books with standardized designs, this may be a satisfactory arrangement, but because the point of view of the production manager is quite different from that of the designer, it is usually not conducive to the highest quality of book design, any more than it is conducive to good architecture for the architect to be responsible to the building contractor.

Indeed, book design is much like architecture. Like architecture, it is a servant art. Like architecture, it offers opportunities for genuine and original artistic expression, and like architecture, it must develop its aesthetic qualities within practical restraints of economy and with a view to ultimate use. In fact very often the aesthetic quality of a beautiful book is an expression of its ultimate use, a handsome configuration of type and margins, inviting to the reader, with suggestive or allusive decorative touches. Visual material related to the subject of a book, whether contemporary or historical, can enhance its appearance if used with subtlety and taste. The designer, however, must always remember that the book is not simply a vehicle for his design; it is to be read by a reader who is primarily interested in the content of the book itself, and the designer should stimulate this interest without coming between the author and the reader.

That is, except for a feeling that a book is attractive and handsome, a reader should not be continually conscious of the design; the design must submerge itself in the experience of reading.

The prime requisite of the designer, beyond an aesthetic sense, is that he know printing and types. His job is to write the specifications for the physical object that is to be created from the manuscript, namely, the book as a whole and in all its parts: title page and front matter, chapter heads, text, illustrations, appendixes, index, paper, binding, and jacket. He must design the book to fit the machines that will manufacture it, keeping in mind limitations of cost. He must know and understand these factors in order to control them, in the production of an object that will be aesthetically satisfying and appropriate to its subject. This is a difficult task, and problems of cost are constantly in conflict with aesthetic ideals. Compromises must often be made, but sometimes the practical stringencies of cost and the limitations of production techniques produce design solutions that are superior to those developing from less stringent situations. It is a question of balance.

There is no point in having an excellent design department unless it can have a certain degree of freedom, but every design department must somehow, in spite of the requirements of art and the inconstancy of inspiration, exist in the internal environment of a publishing house, with relationships to the editorial, production, and marketing departments, and it must work within restrictions of time and cost.

The Production Department

The production department buys composition, paper, printing, and binding, according to specifications it gets from the design department. Few publishers have their own printing plants; and even when they do, the production and printing departments are usually organized separately so that one buys printing from the other. The scheduling requirements of the production department may be impossible for the printing department to satisfy, and most publishers prefer the flexibility that comes from buying printing from outside suppliers. Therefore the usual production department has many relationships with various printers and binders, getting bids and letting contracts, in addition to watching schedules and routing proofs, checking invoices and comparing costs with estimates, and so forth. The production department is interested in quality, speed, and economy—three usually conflicting goals, so compromises have to be made. As in so many other aspects of publishing, it is a question of balance.

Everybody—the author, the editor, the designer, the marketing manager, and the publisher—wants to get the book out quickly, or at least on a definite and usually rather tight schedule. But speed costs money and is often attained only at a sacrifice of quality. And everybody wants quality; nobody is satisfied with a book that is poorly printed and bound. And everybody wants economy; the publisher wants it because it is *his* money that is being spent, and the author and editor and designer and marketing department all hope the price (which is *somehow* related to cost; see Chapter IV) will not be too high.

The production manager's job is a center of conflict. The manager is inherently under various pressures, and he cannot possibly satisfy everyone. Even in a small publishing house there may be fifty or one hundred or more books (including reprints) in various stages of production at any one time. The size of the department will depend mainly on the number of new titles and reprints issued each year. New titles are constantly coming in with requested production schedules and with specifications that may be difficult to fill. The production manager and his department must keep track of a thousand details. They must maintain contact with various printers and binders, constantly worrying about costs and quality, and constantly adjusting schedules that are unfortunately often broken by printers, designers, editors, and authors. Of course there are always reasons, and usually good reasons, why schedules are broken. The author was ill or traveling and couldn't read the proofs on time. A new discovery required revision of a scientific work. Printing must be delayed or advanced to meet a book club's schedule. The editor or designer was ill or on vacation. The printer could not meet his schedule because his plant is overloaded and additional help is not available. And so forth.

The production department tries to maintain an orderly flow of work, and it tries to maintain standards of quality while holding costs down and keeping schedules, but it is a constant battle. Crisis follows crisis, and to the production manager it often appears that impossible demands are being made on him. In this he is correct, and he must recognize and to some degree accept this situation. He and his department must not only handle the thousands of details required to schedule the manufacturing of hundreds of books at a reasonable cost; they must also have a broad enough knowledge of the publishing house to sense priorities, or if they can't decide on priorities, they must consult the publisher. Then they must be able to explain to those who want the impossible that the impossible cannot be achieved—and why—and they must have convincing reasons.

To do this exceedingly difficult job the production department must be highly organized. Some one person has the primary responsibility of keeping track of schedules, noting the times at which the various stages of production are due to be completed (manuscript to printer, galleys to editor, galleys to printer, pages to editor, etc.), and following every book through the schedule, recording actual times of completion, checking when something is late, readjusting schedules as necessary. Someone coordinates the flow of work to outside suppliers, maintaining good working relationships while preserving a competitive situation. Someone works up estimates and checks costs. Someone orders paper and cloth and other needed materials, trying to get the advantage of bulk prices while keeping inventory down. Someone, probably the production manager himself, checks quality, and of course he supervises the entire activity.

And the exasperating thing is that everyone's attention is always focused on the rush book, or on some book that is causing problems. No one notices the hundreds of books that go through smoothly, on schedule, without difficulties.

The Marketing Department

The marketing department, like the editorial department, is in direct touch with the external environment. Its job is to get books to readers, and it must know who and where the potential readers are, and how they can be reached, but usually only a small proportion of the books go directly from the publishing house to the readers. Most books go through wholesalers and bookstores and libraries, and publishers of educational books at the elementary and high school levels sell mainly to school systems. Only a few kinds of publishing houses (subscription books, encyclopedias, book clubs) sell a large proportion of their books directly to the ultimate readers.

Thus the marketing department must carry on a variety of activities—to sell the books to the wholesalers, booksellers, libraries, and school systems, and to make the readers want the books. The focus of the marketing department's energy must be where the decision to buy the book is made, and this will vary depending on the type of book and on the particular individual book. Teachers, for example, must be informed about new educational books, and the most effective way to do this is to give them copies of the books; if a teacher adopts a book, the school system or the students must buy it. Sometimes thousands of copies of an elementary textbook are given away to teachers, but every adoption can mean a large and continuing sale, and educational publishing can be highly profitable. For the same reason, college teachers are given a large variety of both hardback and paperback books, in the hope that they will put them on required or recommended reading lists. Certain kinds of books are given away to public figures (congressmen, TV personalities, etc.) in the hope that they will mention them in public. And books are sent to review media and to reviewers for the obvious purpose of reviewing.

Apparently the principal method of selling books is to give them away, and perhaps it is the most effective method. But it is also an expensive method, and one must be reasonably sure that a certain number of books will be sold for every one given away. In certain fields, such as technical or university press publishing, where editions tend to be small and the potential readership is limited, the number of free copies must be carefully controlled. Copies go only to carefully selected review media and perhaps a few experts who may endorse the book in advertising. Any free distribution beyond that is not only costly but also a possible sale lost from a limited market.

But one way or another, the potential readers must be informed about each new book, and all the various advertising techniques are used: space advertising in newspapers and magazines and specialized journals; direct mail advertising to appropriate mailing lists; exhibiting at appropriate specialized or public meetings; or, for a very general book such as a cookbook or jokebook, TV and radio advertising may be attempted. Publicity of various kinds will be sought: news releases are sent out, author interviews are arranged, and the book trade is informed through advance information in trade publications. Advertising will be directed to the book trade as well as to potential readers, so that bookstores and libraries can order well in advance of publication.

In the book trade itself, salesmen play a vital function, visiting bookstores and wholesalers regularly and keeping them informed about forthcoming books. A good salesman will know each bookstore and its customers, and will be able to advise the buyer how many of each title he should order before publication. The salesman will also check stock against the backlist and recommend reorders. To do this he must know how many of each title the store ordered on his previous visit, and since; this means a lot of record keeping, but it is essential. If books are in the store, they may be seen and bought. If they are not, the reader who finds out about them elsewhere will then request the bookseller to put in an order—a long and tedious chain which is often broken.

It is not reasonable, however, to expect most bookstores to stock more than a limited selection of current books, popular paperbacks, and classics, although there are some bookstores that specialize in scientific and technical books, for example. But in the United States over 30,000 new books are published every year, to say nothing of a slightly greater number of books in English published in Great Britain, plus many thousands of foreign books that might be wanted by an American reader. Even a trade publisher whose books would normally be stocked in bookstores where they can be seen and bought on impulse will need to inform potential readers directly, through advertising or publicity. Other publishers advertise to persuade readers to order the book either through a bookstore or directly.

The marketing department must be organized to sell in this complex market. It will have salesmen who make regular visits to wholesalers and booksellers. It will have experts at direct mail and space advertising. Someone will be responsible for publicity, including sending review copies to the right media and free copies to the right influential people. The department may have a library specialist; certainly a major effort in space and direct mail advertising will be intended for libraries. And all this activity will be supervised by the marketing manager.

These various kinds of promotion and selling activity do not go on independently. The potential readership for each book must be considered, and an advertising, sales, and promotion program developed especially for it. There is a budget, of course, and the program must be made to fit the budget. The marketing manager watches advance orders from bookstores and wholesalers, and in consequence he may adjust the budget. After the book is published, he analyzes sales and the reports from salesmen visiting bookstores. The advertising budget may then be increased or cut back, though usually it is too late to do much cutting.

Also, if a book is not selling well, do you do more advertising or less? It is a matter for judgment in a particular situation. The marketing manager checks sales of current books and backlist books, watches the effects of selling and advertising, and, drawing on his earlier experience, directs new efforts.

The marketing manager and his department deal with the external environment. To do this effectively they must be in constant communication with the internal environment of the publishing house. Why is the firm publishing this particular book? Who was it written for? What does the editor think of it, and what recommendations does he have? Are outside expert opinions available, and may they be quoted in advertising? Are there any special design features? Illustrations? What visual material is available for advertising? When can we see galleys and read the book ourselves? What will the jacket be like? When is the scheduled publication date and will the book really make it? The advertisements must be scheduled in relation to the publication date. How many printed pages? What price and what discount will apply? Are there any special book club or other deals?

It is evident that the marketing department must be in close touch with every other department, receiving information from them and also relaying to them attitudes, opinions, and information from the external environment. What do the booksellers say about the design of our books, or about our prices, or about our performance in shipping and billing? What is their attitude toward our discount policy? our returns policy? Are the libraries satisfied with our bindings? What are the specialists saying at our exhibits at professional meetings? Did we lose sales because a certain book was published too near Christmas? And so forth.

Feedback from the marketing department to the other departments is important in all kinds of publishing, and it is often strangely neglected or even resented. One occasionally finds the attitude, "It's our job to make the books; now you salesmen get out there and sell them." A publishing house with sales-oriented editors may even find this attitude successful, though such editors are not likely to ignore reverberations in the sales department. Some publishing houses operate with a large degree of insulation between the editors and the marketing department, and some editors consider themselves a kind of intellectual elite, who should not be much concerned with selling. Perhaps this is necessary since editors must come in many shapes and personalities to deal with a variety of authors, but when it happens something is lost. A successful publishing house is not an assemblage of independent, disconnected departments; it is a structure with many doors, some opening in, others out. If some of the doors are locked, the house will not function harmoniously or well.

In discussing the work of the editorial, design, production, and marketing departments, we have emphasized the importance of

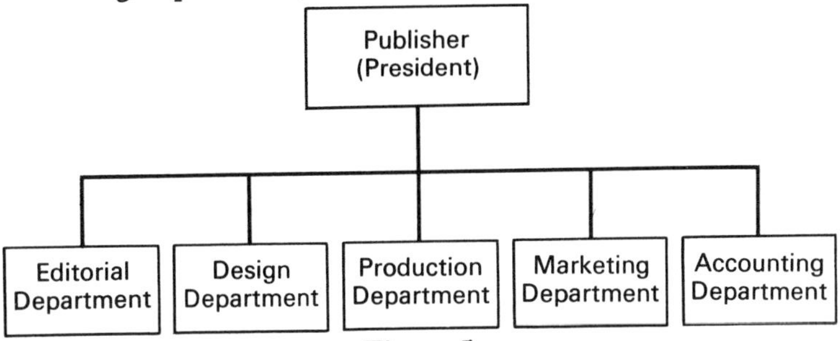

Figure 5

communication, both internal and external, in carrying out their functions. Every department must communicate with every other department, in addition to doing its own job. This takes time and requires effort, but it is essential. To a large extent, this communication can be carried out by department heads as part of their managerial duties, but it should be understood by everyone in every department, and there are many occasions when individual editors and designers and production men and salesmen have opportunities to improve performance by communicating directly. Orderly organization in the complex process of publishing is essential, but such organization applies mainly to responsibility and job assignments, and it should not prevent or restrict interdepartmental communication. For this reason we have avoided the conventional block diagram showing lines of responsibility and authority, but for contrast we will give it here (Figure 5). The trouble with this diagram is that it does not show how anything works. Figure 4 is a little better, but still not very satisfactory. Figure 6, showing the four operating depart-

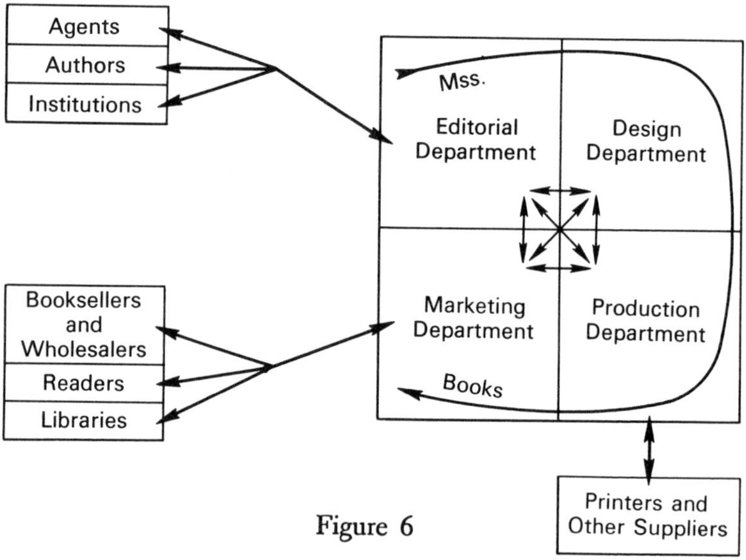

Figure 6

ments just described, gives a somewhat more realistic picture. The double-headed arrows in the center and to the external environment indicate two-way communication. The circular arrow indicates work flow from manuscripts to books, though actually this is a much more complex process which we shall discuss later. Meanwhile it would almost seem from the diagram that a publishing house could exist with just four departments, and indeed it could, if it weren't for the two M's, money and management—or, if you like, the two C's, cash and coordination.

The Accounting Department

We have talked a great deal about the flow of information among departments, but the accounting department is the compiler and source of certain kinds of essential information. The accounting department is involved with the publishing process at every stage, and though the work of getting a book published does not flow *through* the accounting department, its contribution to the control and regulation of publishing activity by the allocation of funds is vital. Moreover, once a book is published, the accounting department is responsible for processing orders and controlling credit, so it becomes an essential part of the distribution function. In addition it (or sometimes the production department) may control the actual storage and shipping of books, which in its detail is a surprisingly complex and interesting operation.

The accounting department is usually thought of as a "service department," and that is what it ought to be. But its services are so essential and the information it generates is so important and revealing about the state of the publishing activity that sometimes it becomes an operating and even a managing department. When this happens, decisions are made that look right from an accounting point of view but may not be right from an overall publishing point of view. Management by accountants is a danger that every head of a publishing house must recognize, at the same time keeping in mind the value of warnings from his cost-minded accountants.

This is not the place for an exposition of the science of accounting, even if I were able to give one. Accounting is a highly complex technical subject taught in special schools, and regulated by law to the extent that certain records must be kept for tax and other purposes. One of the characteristics of accounting is that it can be applied to any business, and publishing, in addition to being other things, is a business. In the publishing business, the accounting department provides the past and current financial information that is necessary to control the business and, in most cases, make a profit. It provides a balance sheet showing the firm's assets and liabilities, a kind of X ray of the constitution of the firm at any given moment. It provides an operating statement showing what the firm has done (in terms of dollars) during the course of the fiscal year; that is, it shows how money was spent, what money was taken in, and how much profit or loss resulted. With the help of the other department heads and in consultation with the manager, it helps to plan the future in the form of a yearly budget. It compares dollar figures and percentages with the budget and with experience from previous years, and it makes comparisons of the firm's performance with the industry as a whole or with an appropriate part of the industry.

The accounting department analyzes the costs of parts of the operation (the editorial department, the marketing department, the general and administrative expenses, and so forth) in great detail, pointing out increases or decreases and variations from previous experience. It prepares other special studies and projections of specific projects as needed. It prepares long-range forecasts (three to five years) of operating results and financial position, which enable the management to predict future financial requirements, answering such questions as how much cash will be needed and when, and when and how much cash will be generated for reinvestment, payment of debt, or dividends. It compares these forecasts with actual experience. It watches the condition of operating cash and inventory investment, and it arranges financing with banks if necessary. It keeps sales records and pays royalties to authors. It pays other bills, such as printers' bills, after making sure that they are correct. It manages the firm's payroll and fringe benefits and general insurance, and keeps contracts and leases. It supplies information of various kinds, regularly or as requested, to all other departments and to the publisher. It prepares tax returns and other reports required by law. In sum, the accounting department performs the traditional accounting function under the special circumstances of the publishing business.

The accounting department works closely with the publisher. In larger firms there will be, in addition to the operating head of the accounting department, a controller, who is the chief financial officer of the firm and who is not involved very much in the day-to-day operation of the accounting department. The controller (or the chief accountant in smaller firms) will keep himself informed as to the current position and progress of the firm and will continually provide projections of the future in relation to the firm's long-range plans and goals. He will plan the financing of major new undertakings, and he will see what special studies need to be made—and make them or see that they are made. He helps to establish financial policies, and he makes or approves operating policies within the accounting department. His job is to see the financial implications of whatever the firm does, and to keep the publisher informed.

In another chapter we will consider in more detail the financial aspects of publishing, but the purpose here is to outline the functions of the accounting department in relation to other departments and to the external environment. It is evident that the accounting department must get much of its information about activities and plans from other departments. It is equally evident that the accounting department supplies essential information to the various departments (e.g., sales statistics to the marketing department). Its budgeting function automatically sets goals and provides a certain degree of control and coordination among the operating departments. In its order-processing and credit-controlling functions, the accounting department is in touch with the external environment, especially bookstores. Thus this department encompasses and pervades the activity of the entire company; although outside the flow of the publishing process, it affects the process profoundly through the information that it acquires, organizes, and provides.

The Office of the Publisher

If each of the departments is performing its function as described in the preceding pages, what is there left for the publisher to do? Ideally, perhaps, he would sit back and watch and supervise, smoking his pipe and looking wise, reading reports and going to occasional meetings, making only the highest policy decisions. Unfortunately, the publisher's life is not like that—or, I suppose, fortunately, since that would not be a very interesting occupation. A publishing house is too complex an organism and the external environment is too changing and varied to permit such a stable existence.

The publisher is of course the manager of the publishing house and is responsible for all its activities. His office, which probably includes some staff assistants, is the coordinating center. He must view the interactions of the various departments and balance and direct their activities, and he probably does this through a management committee consisting of the heads of the departments with himself as chairman with decision-making power. He will also work individually with department heads on problems within their departments. He will try to take an overall view, tempering the conflicting requirements and desires of the different departments with a sense of what is best for the house as a whole. In doing this the publisher must be sensitive to the external environment: to the authors and agents and institutions and booksellers and wholesalers and libraries and readers and printers and binders and banks with which the house has direct relations. He will be sensitive to competition from other publishing houses and in the book market, and he will be aware of new ideas and trends that may affect the book industry. The publisher's office is the center of decision- and policy-making. No work actually flows through his office; it comes to his office for approval or is carried out on the basis of policies and procedures approved by him. The publisher's experience and judgment and knowledge are applied to the program as a whole or to specific areas as appropriate or as needed, always with the overall goals of the publishing house in mind.

The publisher himself probably reports to a board of directors or similar governing body. With that body he sets the goals of the house, which may be profit- or mission-oriented but which in fact are nearly always some combination of the two. Most publishing houses must make a profit, but most publishers do not see themselves simply as businessmen; they are aware of and take satisfaction in their social and cultural role, and they will not publish just *anything* that will make money.

Each publisher within his own house sets standards and goals and conveys these to his staff through his own actions and decisions and through his personal style. The style of the publisher, in a general sense, is inevitably communicated to his personnel and to some extent adopted by them, and many of their actions and decisions grow out of this style, either directly or indirectly. This almost undefinable area of leadership deeply affects morale and performance. There is no single style that is recognized as uniquely effective or appropriate; style grows out of the personality of the publisher and is modified by the personalities of his associates and the goals and environment of his house. The style of a house will change from time to time, especially if a new publisher takes charge or if new goals are set, though such change is not likely to occur rapidly.

With the functions of the accounting department and the publisher's office in mind, we may return to Figure 6, and we will see that in order to represent properly the relations of these two activities to the operating departments a third dimension will be required. The four operating departments can be shown as rectangular blocks surrounded by two collars, one of which is accounting and the other management (see Figure 7). At the front of the structure the editorial and marketing departments have direct contact with the external environment of authors

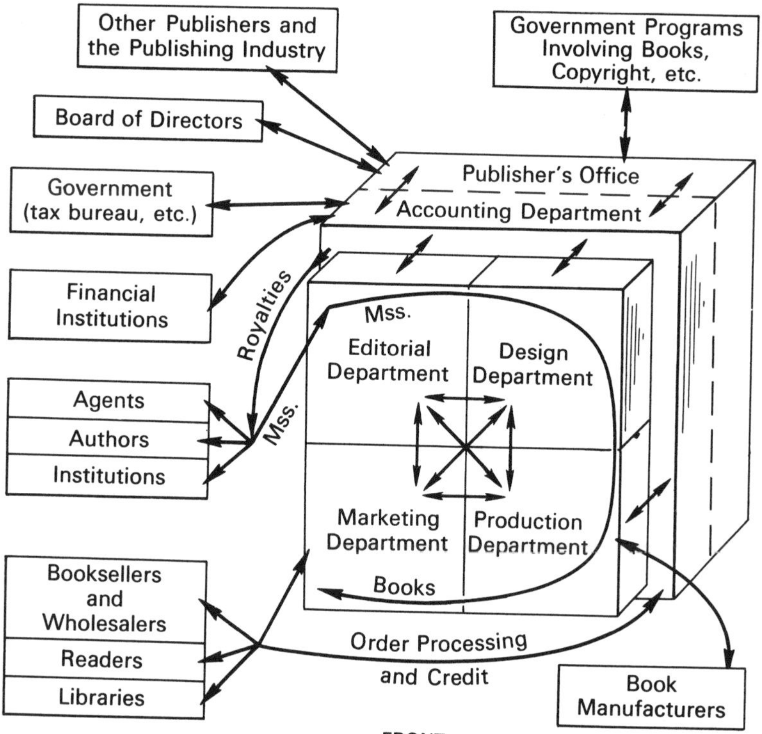

FRONT

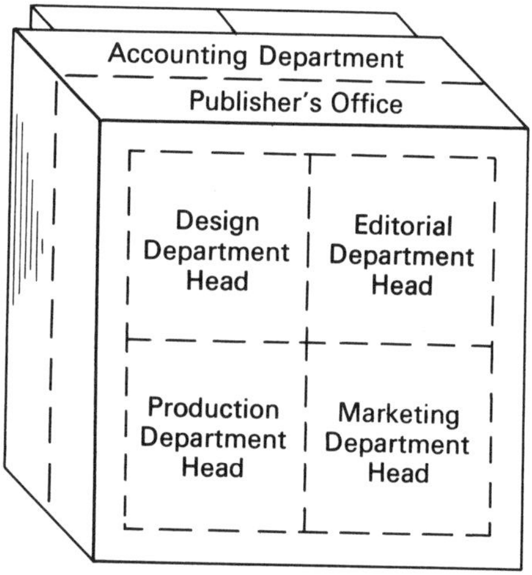

Figure 7

BACK

and readers, and the production and accounting departments also have their specialized external relationships. At the back of the structure the blocks merge (as indicated by dotted lines), as the department heads join with the publisher in the management function. The publisher himself has contact with every activity and function, though he does not normally participate in their daily work.

Figure 7 does not, of course, say anything that has not been said in the preceding discussion. It is simply an attempt to depict graphically the relations among various parts of a publishing house. It might be used as a model against which any actual publishing house could be checked. A large house with several divisions might assume one of the forms shown in Figure 8.

It is symbolic that in larger publishing houses it is harder both graphically and in practice to maintain the close contact between departments—for example, between the editorial and marketing departments, as indicated in Figures 8*b* and 8*c*. Communication becomes increasingly dependent upon the department heads, who merge with management at the back of the diagram. And of course each division will probably have its own manager, which isolates the individual departments still further from the merged departments. One might think that the situation shown in Figure 8*a* would be better, and it has some real advantages, but the advantages of closer coordination within each division must be balanced against the efficiencies and economies that are possible in carrying out production and marketing on a large scale. Various large publishers meet these problems in different ways, attempting to get economies of scale without losing coordination.

The schematic Figures 7 and 8 should perhaps be drawn with wavy lines; certainly the structure should not be and usually is not a rigid one. Specialization and organization within a publishing house are necessary, but flexibility is necessary too, to meet changing conditions in the environment and to accommodate changing internal situations. The analogy with an organism in its environment is quite relevant, and a publishing house is somewhat like one of the higher organisms. In a changing and sometimes harsh environment, a simple organism like a jellyfish can survive only because it is so simple; it drifts and is subjected to the environment, carrying on only the most elementary activities. But higher organisms such as mammals carry on an enormous variety

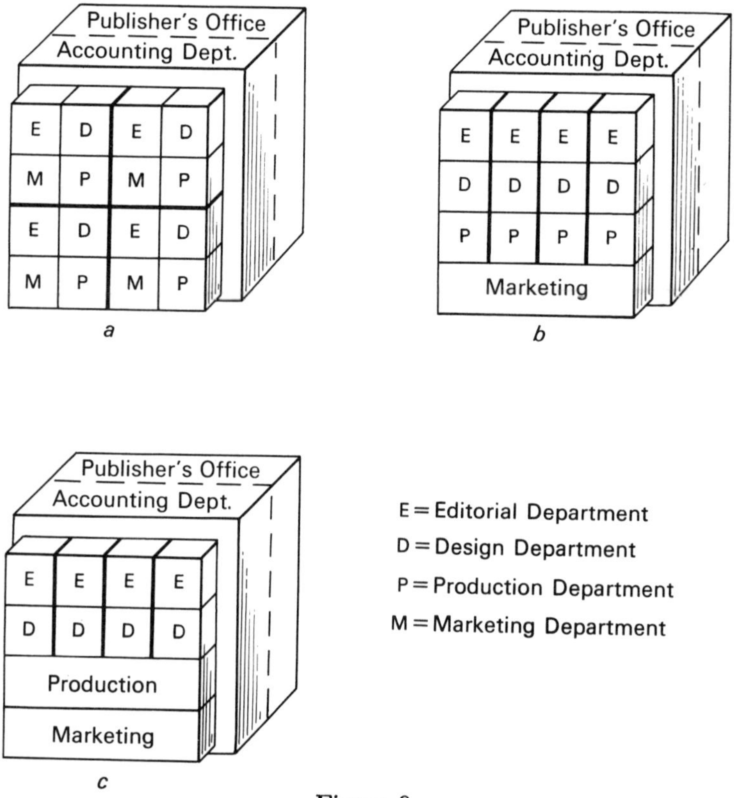

Figure 8

of activities in widely varying environments, often changing the environment to make it more hospitable and in any case maintaining a highly organized internal environment that is kept stable by controlled responses to the external environment. The nervous system, centered at the brain, provides a control mechanism that reaches to every part of the organism, sensing the environment and stimulating appropriate reactions, but the nervous system itself does not carry out any actions; those are performed by limbs with muscular energy. Moreover the higher organisms can learn from experience, either developing reflexes or storing historical information in the brain, and this experience can be applied and adapted to new situations.

But this analogy should not be pushed too far. It must be remembered that a publishing house is not simply an organization—it is an aggregation of individual people organized for a common purpose, but the people retain their individual personalities and abilities and purposes that are separate from those of the publishing house. One of the prime responsibilities of the management, and especially of the publisher himself, is the selection and continuing performance of people.

PEOPLE IN PUBLISHING

We have looked at the tasks and relations of the various departments of a publishing house, and we have examined the publisher's role, with his department heads, of communicating a style and approach and attitude that will enhance performance and morale. It is exceedingly difficult to say how this role is carried out. Performance is affected by the look on the publisher's face when he walks into the office in the morning, by the way he speaks and responds to his colleagues and to junior staff members, by the tone of the letters and memoranda he writes, by the way meetings are conducted, by the degree to which people are allowed to share in important decisions, and by the way recognition for success is granted, and so forth. It depends ultimately on the way the publisher views his own job and on his attitude toward his colleagues as individuals. Publishing undoubtedly is a very important part of his life, but however much the publisher devotes himself to his work, he must view his colleagues as individuals, not just as functioning members of his organization. The formal organization can often be stretched or bent to let a man do what he can do best, and to avoid requiring him to do what he dislikes or is not good at. Of course there are limits to how tolerant the publisher can be; the publishing job must be done, and done well. It will be done well if the publisher can communicate his goals and attitudes to the staff, and if he has chosen a staff that has the right combination of abilities and personalities.

A beginner in publishing should be concerned about the kind of publishing house he is joining more than about the particular job in it, because it is possible to move from activity to activity within publishing, especially if the publisher and department heads are interested in the development of beginners—which is a normal and essential part of their jobs. A wise publisher or department head will do his best to give his staff a variety of publishing experience and will move people from job to job according to their preferences and abilities, so far as possible. This year's beginners are next year's experts. They are the potential replacements for more experienced people who may leave or retire, or they may fill new jobs that may be created as the house develops and grows.

If you look at the composition of personnel of most publishing houses you will find:

(1) some beginners, just learning one aspect or specialty;

(2) some experienced personnel and "old pros" who are expert in one aspect and have some knowledge of other aspects;

(3) department heads, who know their own fields well and have a broad knowledge of publishing; and

(4) the publisher and his immediate staff.

At a glance one sees that specialization decreases as one moves from category (1) to category (4). The specialists in category (2) do the bulk of the work of the house. If they have been chosen or trained well, they may know more about their specialties than the department heads and they certainly should have more specialized knowledge than the publisher. The publisher may have come up through one of the departments, usually editorial or marketing or sometimes accounting, but he cannot be an expert in all aspects of publishing. He must have confidence in and depend on the specialists, and his contribution must come through his direction of their activity in the light of his broader view and of his knowledge of the particular situation and goals of the publishing house.

Recently there has been much concern about training for publishing, caused mainly by the rapid expansion of the book industry and the realization of the need for more capable people at all levels. The problem is to some degree a question of salary levels; publishing has always been an attractive occupation, partly because of the widespread interest in books and partly because of the prestige that is associated with publishing, and one result has been a lag in salary levels behind those for comparable positions in other industries. But publishing has now become big business—at least for some publishers—and the competition for many kinds of publishing talent is great.

Training programs for publishing jobs would increase the supply and perhaps reduce the competition—and possibly the people trained and hired would be more efficient, and there would be less of a need for in-service training programs with consequent costs and demands on the time of busy people. The American Book Publishers Council and the Association of American University Presses have concerned themselves with this problem, as has the Publishers Association in England, where the Booksellers Association has led the way. There is a lot that can be learned about publishing in a short course such as that given each summer at Radcliffe College, but I do not have much faith in the more elaborate and ambitious courses that are being planned in some quarters. Publishing is not an intellectual discipline like mathematics or political science or classical studies; it is an activity and a process. The degree to which it can be abstracted and presented in a meaningful way in a formal course is very limited; as in tennis or golf, you can learn a certain amount from books or lectures, but pretty soon you have to get out and swing at the ball. Then good coaching will help, but only the participant can improve his swing.

So good people must be brought into publishing the way they are brought into other businesses. The opportunities must be attractive and must be made known. Able people, intelligent and motivated and with good educational background, must be selected and challenged and advanced in salary and responsibility. This will be a task for the publishers' associations, for each publishing house, and especially for the managers who hire and promote within the house.

There are many things a publishing house can do internally, aside from salaries and fringe benefits, to make jobs attractive, and internal benefits have a way of becoming known to job applicants. Moreover a good internal program of training and advancement will enhance the attitudes and performance of all the staff, improving morale and encouraging professionalism. Here are some possibilities:

1. Include a job category of "trainee" for beginners, and make special efforts to give trainees a variety of experience under expert guidance.

2. Let each department, or several departments together, conduct a series of seminars, on company time, covering various aspects of publishing. Such seminars can be very useful in interdepartmental communication as well as for training, and the old hands may benefit as much as the new ones. Moreover the staff members who prepare material for presentation in seminars will be forced to review and organize their practices, a worthwhile exercise that may lead to improvements.

3. Encourage staff members to participate in the various publishers' formal and informal groups such as the Publishers' Ad Club, the Permissions Managers' Group, the Editors' Lunch Group, the Children's Book Council.

4. Send staff members to formal meetings of the publishers' associations, especially where there are relevant panel discussions and presentations, and also to some of the special sessions on specific topics such as accounting, market analysis, production methods, and so forth. Encourage them to participate on committees of the associations and if possible help to get them appointed to such committees.

5. Give younger members a chance to make presentations of their own at departmental meetings or seminars; the old hands haven't thought of everything.

6. Encourage staff members to write for the trade journals.

It would be possible to extend this enumeration, but the most important aspect of the above items is that such activities indicate an attitude of the publisher toward his staff. A staff working in such an atmosphere will be trying to improve its performance, will take pride in its accomplishments, and will use more energy and imagination than one that simply does what it is told and is completely occupied with the operating details of the immediate job at hand. Such a staff will be constantly improving itself, and when a staff member leaves, there will be others on the staff who can move up into his job. It almost goes without saying that whenever possible one should promote from within, and with the right kind of staff-development program this should almost always be possible.

Managers should certainly not be afraid to let staff members expose themselves at trade association meetings lest they be hired away. It makes sense to fight to keep a good man, but not to hide him. Good people will not permit themselves to be hidden and will leave sooner if an attempt is made to do so. And if someone on the staff moves on to a better job in another firm, that provides opportunity and encouragement to those remaining. In fact, it sometimes proves advantageous to lose a good man, in spite of the loss, on account of the resulting opportunities for realignment of work and advancement in the staff. The quality of a small house can almost be measured by the number of its alumni in high places in other publishing houses. A small house with a stable top management must expect a certain flow of personnel at the lower and middle levels, simply because the top jobs are filled, and it is an advantage to such a house to become known as "a good place to be from." That is, it is a place where young people can improve their knowledge and experience under expert guidance, and it is a place where other publishers look when trying to fill an important position. Such a firm will attract a stream of talent, and while the managers probably fret over the loss of personnel and the problem of training new people, there will be the offsetting advantage of new energy and new ideas that come with each new person.

In sum, we have looked first at the external environment of a publishing house, then we have examined the internal organization of a typical house in its operating and managerial functions, and finally we have considered the individual people who perform various publishing tasks. We have gone from the general to the particular, and it is appropriate to end this section with the idea that, no matter how it is organized, a publishing house cannot be any better than the people who constitute its staff and whose activities constitute its life. I do not refer simply to the quality of the staff's publishing skills, though such skills are essential, but to the quality of the people on the staff as people. Publishing is an important part of their lives, and the publishing house and its books are an expression of their work. Their quality as individuals, entirely aside from their skills, will be reflected in the house as a whole, as it plays its part in the life of our larger society.

III

FLOWS, SEQUENCES, AND DECISIONS

We have discussed the external and internal environments of a publishing house—the authors, readers, and other outside influences and the internal organization and coordination—much as if a publishing house were an organism. Indeed that analogy has been drawn, and we have attempted to picture the organism as it exists in a kind of equilibrium with its environments, external and internal. But obviously a publishing house is not in static equilibrium; its environments are constantly changing and it must constantly adjust its functioning or cease to exist. There must be a continuous flow of energy (new books, money) to keep the publishing house alive, and decisions must be made to control this flow.

In the course of time a publishing house changes. These changes may be in response to the external environment (ideas of authors, changes in the educational system, new technologies, competition, tastes of readers, etc.) or to internal changes (new personnel, new editorial ideas, new policies, new financial control, etc.). A primary task of publishing management is to control change—not to inhibit change, since change is necessary for survival—and often management must stimulate change. In any case change must be controlled and directed by making a variety of large and small decisions, constantly adjusting actions in the light of short- and long-term experience and in relation to conscious goals.

The ultimate goal may be a certain level of return on investment, or a desired growth factor, or propagation of certain ideas, or publishing support of educational or research activity, or some combination of these or other goals, but the ultimate goal will be expressed in terms of more specific short-term decisions: to publish a certain number of new books this year, to maintain inventories at a certain level, to achieve a certain level of sales performance, to publish certain individual books or types of books. These decisions are made for a definite time, perhaps in relation to a yearly budget, and then are reevaluated and made again. Decisions on the acceptance of manuscripts are made periodically during the year in relation to an overall yearly budget of acceptance. Major decisions on advertising budgets are probably made twice a year, once for each of the two publishing seasons (spring and fall; publishing has only two selling seasons)* in relation to a yearly budget that may be adjusted during the year. Numerous detailed decisions must be made about each individual book: on acceptance and contract terms, on editorial problems, on format, on price, on quantity to print, on marketing strategy, and so forth. All the detailed decisions regarding individual books merge to constitute the total publishing result, the life of the publishing house, so the overall publishing decisions must provide the context in which the individual decisions are made.

MACRO-PUBLISHING AND MICRO-PUBLISHING

To a large extent, the management of a publishing house is like other business management, and many of the rules and practices that apply to other businesses apply equally to publishing. One has, for example, similar problems of capital investment,

* A few houses recognize three seasons, spring, summer, and fall.

control of inventories, cash flow, credit, personnel, administrative organization, and so forth. Publishers can learn much from the textbooks of business management, and indeed some successful publishers have come to publishing from other businesses, but there is a reluctance to recognize this similarity because there is a feeling that "publishing is different because books are different." Accountants and management consultants who may be called in to help with particular problems are always told first that "publishing is not like other businesses," as a kind of warning that their standard rules and procedures will not apply. And there is a reason for this: although in many ways publishing is a business like other businesses, publishing is indeed different from most other businesses.

Publishing is different, first, because of its cultural aspects. Publishers for the most part are very conscious of the cultural role of books of all kinds, and often their decisions are based as much on literary or other cultural aspects as on business judgment. The best editor, even from a business point of view, may be one who has a sense of style or a feeling for the public pulse rather than any conscious concern for business aspects. Although the publisher's social function may be defined as the support and diffusion of culture through books by business methods, business methods may sometimes be looked down on or neglected. Some publishers and publishing houses are clearly much more business-minded than others, as we have seen in the chapter on publishing objectives; nevertheless, few are motivated only by considerations of financial gain.

But there is another way in which "publishing is different." Each new book (or integrated series of books) is a new venture; in a sense it is a new business, involving many of the same but also many different considerations from the business as a whole. A publisher produces a "list" of books, each of which must be nurtured, considered for publication, contracted for, edited, designed, manufactured, and sold. Each book has many individual characteristics that affect its progress at every stage. It has a different author and different readers (a different market). It requires an independent and separate decision to proceed with publication, a decision often based on only a very small amount of information—the judgment or taste of a few editors and some hunches about its probable reception by the public. At any rate, whatever the basis of the decision to publish, a whole sequence of subsequent decisions must be made about preparation, packaging (design), manufacturing (including size of edition), and marketing, as if that book were a separate business.

At this point, for convenience and not to invoke any pseudoscientific atmosphere, I want to introduce some new terms, namely "macro-publishing" and "micro-publishing." *"Macro-publishing" includes all those aspects which involve the publishing house and its list as a whole; "micro-publishing" includes those considerations that are involved in decisions about an individual book.* I am aware that these are awkward terms, but they are descriptive, and none of the more customary terms seem to be quite right. Instead of "macro-publishing," for example, one might use "general publishing," but that term is often used to mean "trade publishing" or other than specialized publishing (e.g., scientific or educational). For "micro-publishing" one might say "title publishing," but this is also awkward and does not have a natural opposite. Also, the terms macro-publishing and micro-publishing exhibit a suggestive parallel with the well-established terms macro-economics (involving the entire economy) and micro-economics (involving only a particular market within the economy). Every publishing house is involved in both macro- and micro-publishing, and one of a publisher's main tasks is to coordinate these two closely related and interesting activities.

One might think that it would be enough to concentrate on micro-publishing, simply to plan a series of individually successful publishing ventures, the total of which would constitute a successful publishing house, but unfortunately this is not true—or in most cases even possible. Individually successful publishing ventures usually require a well-organized and skillfully managed macro-publishing activity to carry them, each title building on the successes of the others and being produced and distributed more efficiently and effectively as a part of a planned list and with the benefit of the attention of a variety of specialists. There are exceptions of course—the chance privately published book that becomes a great popular success; the professor's mimeographed course notes that become a standard work—but most books need, and virtually all can benefit from, a coordinated macro-publishing and micro-publishing effort. Table I gives a partial list of the concerns involved in each area.

TABLE I

Macro-Publishing	*Micro-Publishing*
Editorial policy	Editorial decisions on manuscripts
House editorial style	Copyediting
House design style or policy	Design of individual book
Control of production cost and quality	Arrangements to manufacture a book
Marketing budget and policy	Marketing plan for a book
Analysis and projection of sales of the list	Sales background or projection for a book
Pricing policy	Price of a book
Inventory policy	Print order for a book
Personnel policy and management	Royalty rate
Organization	
Discount structure	Discount category
Budgeting and financial management	
Copyright and rights	Subsidiary rights (e.g., book-club possibilities)

It is evident from Table I that macro-publishing is mainly the responsibility of the top management of a firm. The board of directors or trustees or stockholders will be vitally interested in financial reports, especially the balance sheet and the operating statement, and for the most part these represent macro-publishing aspects. Such boards will want to hear about general questions of editorial policy, such as the entry of the firm into a new field (e.g., juveniles) or the establishment of a new major series. They will be concerned with individual titles only in unusual circumstances (a major best seller, a prize-winning book). Thus the top management of the firm, being ultimately responsible for macro-aspects, will give these matters much attention.

Yet the success of the firm will depend to a large degree on effective micro-publishing—the selection of books to be published, their efficient production, and marketing to particular readerships. In the course of daily work, multitudes of decisions are made in the micro-publishing area as editorial reports are written, manuscripts are accepted and contracts written, designs developed, printing contracts let, and advertising and sales programs projected. The publishing manager must control all these many decisions and activities in the micro-publishing sphere, always with an eye to the macro-publishing results.

There is of course no inherent conflict between macro-publishing and micro-publishing, though micro-publishing decisions will be affected by macro-publishing considerations, since they must fit within the macro-publishing framework. But each area is sufficiently complex, requiring constant attention, so that it will be difficult if not impossible for any one person to work effectively in both areas in a firm of any size. It might be said that macro-publishing is the establishment of policy, and the word "policy" appears many times on the macro-publishing side of Table I; but it is not sufficient just to establish policy and then work within it. Policies must be constantly reviewed in the light of macro-publishing considerations and the needs of the micro-publishing activity, so that macro-publishing itself is an activity and an operation, not static supervision and policing. In each of the two areas there is a kind of flow that must be watched and controlled, and each greatly affects the other. In micro-publishing there is the flow of an individual book through the editorial, design, production, and marketing stages; in macro-publishing there is cash flow, inventory control, investment in operating costs (overhead), and the rate of output in new titles and reprints, all adding up to the control of investment in its many aspects, including investment in personnel.

Thus the macro-publishing manager must become deeply involved in micro-publishing, but not so deeply that he ignores macro-functions. He must constantly watch and review micro-publishing activities, as to quality and quantity and scheduling, adjusting the micro-publishing activity by revising policies, adopting budgets, adding or replacing or reducing personnel, issuing general directives, or occasionally, if necessary, interfering by making decisions in the micro-publishing area. Thus the publisher as such, being the overall manager, must be able when necessary to function in any of the aspects of micro-publishing in order to operate effectively in the area which must be his main concern, namely, macro-publishing.

It is obvious that the publisher, even in a small publishing house, must delegate responsibility and rely on staff members to carry out virtually all of the daily publishing activity. But even the delegation of responsibility has its macro- and micro-publishing aspects. The publisher will delegate responsibility for micro-aspects to the editor and his editorial staff, to the chief designer and his staff, to the production manager and his staff, to the marketing manager and his sales and advertising specialists, and to the order-handling people in the accounting department. In the macro-publishing he will take prime responsibility, as indeed he must ultimately, for the whole publishing house; but he will probably not want to rely entirely on his own judgment and he will probably want to delegate certain macro-publishing areas to other people.

The first and most obvious area for delegation is financial management, which will probably be the main concern of a controller or financial vice-president. In this area he may also have advice from the firm's auditors or from other specialists such as bankers. In other macro-publishing areas, such as personnel, he may delegate operating responsibility, and in a large firm it may be desirable to set up a person or group with "staff functions," that is, with responsibility to study and advise on but not take operating responsibility for various aspects, both macro and micro, but usually with special concern for the firm as a whole. Whether or not there is a formal staff, the publisher will want to keep in close touch with the heads of his operating, or "line," departments, who must understand the macro-aspects in order to perform effectively in micro-areas, and to a large extent they will act as a staff, providing studies in their own areas and advising on macro-aspects.

MICRO-PUBLISHING DECISIONS

Since the macro-publishing outcome is largely the result of all the numerous micro-publishing decisions, let us look first at the sequence of decisions that are made with respect to an individual book and the information on which such decisions are based. This sequence, which has many variations, is outlined in the following numbered items:

1. *To invite submission.* This is usually decided by an editor on the basis of a description of the book, usually in a letter or an outline. An invitation to an author to write the proposed book is often accompanied by a contract with an advance against royalties.

2. *To accept a manuscript for publication.* Except with very well-established authors, final acceptance is nearly always based on editorial reports on a completed or nearly completed manuscript. Before writing the contract the careful publisher will usually want manufacturing-cost estimates and estimates of probable sales based on experience with similar books. It is desirable at this point to work out a tentative publication plan, including print order, price, discount category, royalty rate, advertising budget, and estimated operating costs. This is extensively discussed in Chapter IV.

3. *Subsidiary rights.* The time of acceptance (or even before) is not too soon to begin work on subsidiary rights (book clubs, first and second serial rights, motion pictures and television, paperback and other special editions). Prospective subsidiary-rights income may enhance a publishing project, but a too-early release of some rights (e.g., paperback) may interfere with hardback publication or may result in lower terms than might be obtainable later.

4. *Design.* The format may have been determined in a preliminary way when making a publication plan. The determination of design combines aesthetics with considerations of production efficiency and marketing effectiveness. Many books have special design requirements for illustrations, tables, and the like. The author's preferences will often be taken into account.

5. *Production.* Production decisions will be made on the basis of bids from suppliers, the requirements of schedule and of quality, and previous experience with suppliers.

6. *Marketing.* A detailed plan for space and direct mail advertising, publicity, and selling to the trade will be developed for each book. It will be based on the marketing department's reading of proofs, editorial reports, experience with similar books, and a sense of the market.

7. *Final decision on print order, price, and discount.* It is often wise to review these matters just before the book goes to press, to take advantage of advance reaction in the book trade and later judgments of staff members (especially the marketing department).

8. *To extend or curtail advertising,* on the basis of reviews and bookstore sales after publication.

9. *To reprint* (*or not*), on the basis of current and projected sales. This is extensively discussed in Chapter IV.

10. *To change the price or discount,* on the basis of changes in the market or analysis of actual sales.

The basic decision is of course the decision to publish. If this decision is good in both an editorial and a business sense, some of the other decisons will not be critical. If this decision is bad, the best design and production efforts combined with an efficient and energetic marketing program may not be enough to rescue the project.

The decision to publish may be good editorially but bad in a business sense. The book may be excellent in its intellectual or literary aspects, but if the publisher overestimates sales or underestimates cost he may be heading for trouble. Or in bidding for a good and prospectively popular book, he may make such a heavy investment in advance royalties that he will lose money even on a reasonably good sale. This is not to say that a publisher should accept only books that are expected to show a profit; there are many reasons for publishing money-losing books—to keep an author, to propagate ideas the publisher or his sponsors believe in, to advance knowledge—but if the book will lose money the publisher should, so far as possible, know it in advance and prepare accordingly. He should be able to decide that the benefit of publishing is worth the estimated monetary loss, and he should know where the money is coming from; university presses and other nonprofit publishers make this kind of decision frequently.

Another way in which the decision to publish is good editorially but bad otherwise occurs when macro-publishing aspects are ignored. A book in, say, advanced geology may be excellent taken by itself, but if the house is not publishing other books in advanced geology, it will probably not be able to do a good job of marketing it. On the other hand, if the house is trying to establish a reputation and a program in geology, a few important books could be a nucleus for further development. Or a good book, one that will sell slowly and produce a substantial profit over a period of years, may be accepted; but if accepting it overextends the house financially, tying up funds that are needed for current operations, the macro-publishing result will be unfavorable.

The decision to publish may be good in a business sense but bad editorially. This is more rare, partly because for most commercial publishers, good and bad are closely related to profit and loss. But every publishing house has a reputation to maintain, and unless the house is willing to become one of those shady purveyors of questionable material, a series of money-making books that will not stand honest scrutiny will hurt in the long run. The staff will be demoralized and leave, and better authors will not want their books to appear over the house's imprint. There are publishing houses that will print anything. "Vanity presses" are the worst offenders, for their only stipulation is that the author pay—and he usually pays dearly. There are also the publishers who specialize in near-pornography, obviously pandering to a public seeking titillation in accounts of sex and violence. And of course even the most respected publishers may err in a matter of judgment or taste or may succumb to the temptation of the fast buck. In short, a good decision to publish a book is one that takes full account of both editorial and business aspects at both the micro- and macro-publishing levels.

The most common cause of difficulties at the macro-level is overexpansion. It takes a certain amount of working capital to run a publishing business, and the bigger the business is, the more it takes. At any given time, money is invested in an inventory of unsold books, in advance royalties to authors, in accounts receivable (uncollected bills), in current operating expenses, and in a cash account to meet immediate needs. As a publishing firm expands, it needs more working capital, more money for these everyday operating activities. If it cannot generate this money fast enough from its own profits, it will need to seek it elsewhere, by borrowing from banks or by issuing stock or bonds to the public. Or the house may get needed operating capital by selling itself to a larger company that can supply capital; recently many publishing houses have merged with or been bought by large electronics companies that can supply capital and that have an interest in what they call "the knowledge industry." The electronics companies see the publishing houses not only as sources of profit but also as sources of educational and other "materials" to fill their electronics channels in the future. The publishing houses, for the most part, need the capital and hope that they won't become submerged as mere "materials suppliers." More will be said about publishing in relation to the new technologies in a later chapter.

EDITORIAL FLOW AND MACRO-PUBLISHING DECISIONS

We have seen that the basic decision at the micro-publishing level is to accept a manuscript or project for publication. This is usually thought of as an editorial decision, though much business judgment must be brought to bear, as we shall see in Chapter IV. But each decision to publish a particular manuscript must be thought of in a macro-publishing context. It is the purpose of this section to relate the micro-publishing decision to accept a manuscript to the macro-publishing situation.

The flow of manuscripts into the house, which is vital for the future of the company, is the responsibility of the editorial department. Editors will be searching for manuscripts and initiating projects that will result in books that will meet the needs of the house. Each morning's mail will be eagerly scanned for promising proposals, and there will be a flow of unsolicited manuscripts submitted by hopeful authors. Each house and each editor will develop individual techniques and practices; for example, trade publishers tend to rely heavily on literary agents, while most other kinds of houses do not. Some educational and university publishers develop relationships with university departments or research organizations that provide a steady flow of manuscripts. All houses try to maintain relationships with productive authors, especially those whom they have published previously.

The point here is that the house must have a sufficient flow of publishable manuscripts to maintain its program at a certain level of output and ultimately of sales income. Every part of the publishing house is staffed and organized to achieve a certain level of activity, and since the salaries and other expenses of these departments continue, if the input of new manuscripts falls below this level for more than a short period, there will have to be some painful retrenchment. What tends to happen, therefore, is that the house accepts approximately the number of manuscripts that will fill its capacity, adjusting its standards of acceptance in relation to the incoming flow. If a house is organized to publish one hundred new books a year, it will accept approximately one hundred books from whatever number are submitted, and the quality (by whatever standard) will depend on the editors' ability to attract and select the kinds of manuscripts the house wants to publish.

The more manuscripts (or projects) submitted and the higher their acceptability by the house's standards, the more selective the house can become, and if the selection process is effective, the quality of the list itself will rise. On the other hand, if a house wants to expand its program, it must stimulate a larger flow of acceptable manuscripts from which to choose; otherwise it will just be accepting manuscripts that would previously have been rejected. In periods of expansion quality tends to drop; this is why a wise publisher wishing to expand his list will do so slowly, yielding gradually to pressure from his editorial department for more acceptances. It doesn't hurt a house very much to reject a few manuscripts that it would really like to publish; the publisher can feel confident that such manuscripts will soon be accepted by other publishers. But it can seriously damage a house's reputation and financial health to accept marginal projects in order to fill out a list; these projects usually look less attractive after they are published.

Thus, in order to allow some flexibility in the number of acceptances, a publishing house should be slightly understaffed, always under pressure and scrambling to get the necessary work done. This is a matter for balance and judgment; one shouldn't make impossible demands, and prolonged pressure is bad for morale and may lead to sloppy work. But most people work best under some pressure, and a staff that is challenged can take pride in its achievement. If the pressure or work load is too great, temporary freelance help may relieve the strain during a peak load. Moreover, the requirement of stringent selectivity in acceptances, leading to higher quality, can itself be a morale-building activity, as the entire staff takes pride in the quality of the house's publications.

Effective selectivity itself is not easy to achieve; it is an ongoing process—a flow. One cannot simply collect a year's supply of submissions, perhaps five hundred or a thousand manuscripts, and then select the ones for publication. There is a steady flow of submissions, and decisions must be made. Usually this is done best by having periodic meetings to decide which manuscripts among those ready for decision should be accepted; the others should be rejected—if they are not acceptable now, they probably won't be later. Some manuscripts may of course be sent back for revision and resubmission later, when they will be considered in effect as new manuscripts—but to be fair to the author, this should not be done unless there is strong confidence that the revised manuscript will be acceptable.

Before the periodic editorial meeting at which manuscripts are accepted, a great deal of work will have been done. To begin with, the majority of submitted manuscripts will have been considered and rejected by the editorial staff; only those thought worthy candidates for acceptance should be presented at the meeting. Then the editorial committee (however constituted) or perhaps the publisher himself will make the final selection in relation to a budget of acceptances, a certain number of acceptances per year to be reached over a sequence of perhaps monthly or even weekly meetings, depending on the total number to be accepted and the need for speed of decision. The meetings should be spaced out enough so that each meeting can consider a reasonable number of manuscripts to be selected in competition with each other, perhaps ten to fifteen manuscripts with an acceptance expectancy of ninety percent (the majority having been rejected beforehand); and the meetings should be frequent enough so that decisions can be taken without undue delay. In fact, no matter what the regular procedure is, there must be some way of breaking through it in emergencies; often the best manuscripts—by the best authors—will not wait, and a decision must be made or the project will be lost to another publisher. Such exceptions should be rare and should be justified by their importance and urgency, but they are sometimes necessary.

The editorial committee should be informed about manuscripts to be considered in advance of each meeting, so far as possible. Depending on the nature of the manuscripts, there will be reports of different kinds: opinions of critics or technical advisers (especially for a technical manuscript), a report from the staff editor sponsoring the manuscript, some information on the probable market for the book (if possible from the marketing department, especially if it is a large or especially risky project), and projected costs and income in the form of a publication plan. In order to save time and make discussion more pointed at the decision-making meeting, the committee should have a chance to study this information and prepare questions or reach judgments in advance. Of course it is difficult and sometimes impossible to have all this information available in time for a scheduled meeeing, or at a time when a decision must be made because of pressure from an author or agent. If this is the case, the decision may have to be made with incomplete evidence, supported by publishing experience and judgment and shrewd horseback estimating—unless the decision can be put over until the next meeting.

Who should participate in the decision to accept manuscripts for publication, besides the publisher himself? In large companies the publisher may even delegate this function to a division head, who is in fact the publisher of the juvenile or adult trade division, for example. The chief editor should certainly participate, and in a commercial house the marketing manager may make a major contribution. The design and production departments need not be represented unless there are special problems involving them; their contribution is in the form of manufacturing estimates submitted to the committee. Staff editors who have sponsored individual manuscripts should certainly be present to discuss their own projects, and it may be helpful to have other sponsoring editors sit at least as observers during the process of final selection. Such participation and observation will help them in developing future projects that will be acceptable. It may be wise for the chief financial officer or his representative to be present, at least when large and expensive projects are being considered, though this is not necessary if the budgetary limits (in terms of investment and number of titles) are kept in mind. But by attending, the financial officer, though he may not participate directly in micro-publishing decisions, may pick up information or gain insight into the micro-publishing operations that will help him in his macro-publishing task of financial control.

FLOW THROUGH COPYEDITING, DESIGN, AND PRODUCTION

The decision to publish leads eventually to the copyediting stage, the process of word by word editing that prepares the manuscript for production. The management of the copyediting activity is a process of controlling a flow in relation to the capacity and special abilities of the staff or freelance copyeditors, the requirements of the design and production departments, and a publication schedule that is probably very important. The chief copyeditor must consider these aspects of each manuscript, assigning it to a copyeditor who will be able to solve whatever problems it presents while remaining on good terms with the author, and who will have it ready for design and production in time so that it can be published on schedule—for the Christmas trade, in time for course adoptions, or in coordination with a book-club release, for example.

Copyediting is an essential task of extraordinary variety, for each book has its own special problems. Good copyediting, intelligent and careful and flexible and sensitive, can help enormously in a house's relations with its authors—and bad copyediting can be disastrous. Some publishers have rules of house style; they may be helpful but they are frequently broken. No formula or routine will replace the copyeditor's combination of technical knowledge with sensitivity to the needs of a book and to the personality of the author.

The design department also has a problem of flow, and the designer like the copyeditor can help or hurt the house's relations with an author. The author has a certain visual image of his book —at the very least he hopes it will be green, or perhaps any color *but* green—and the designer should try to meet the author's wishes. Preferably the designer has been assigned to the book while it is still in the copyediting stage, so that at an early stage the editor can confer with him about problems of illustration, tables, headings and subheads, and the like; and the editor can convey the author's preferences. Sometimes the author will come in for a conference, especially if there are major problems of illustration. But besides the author, the designer has other people to please—especially himself. If he is an artist, and he should be, he will have in mind a physical form which to his trained aesthetic sense expresses the particular book—is "right" for it. It is easy to design a routinely legible book, but it takes much thought and pains to produce a beautiful one. A good designer's vision will transcend the author's image of the book, though it may include it; it will employ and evoke the great tradition of bookmaking while providing for each book an individuality that expresses its character and enhances its use. In doing this, the designer must keep in mind the technical requirements of the printer and the need to hold manufacturing costs within a budget. Finally, he must design a book, *and especially a jacket,* that will satisfy the marketing department. Since the book must be sold at a certain list price, the designer probably has general instructions to make it "about three hundred pages," and because of illustrations it may have to be in a large format—and so forth. These requirements will impinge on the designer's vision of the ideal book, and he may either accept them and design within them or try to persuade the publisher or the marketing manager that the book does not have to be three hundred pages. And somehow this aesthetic and practical problem must be solved on schedule, so that production can proceed and publication can be properly timed.

As the chief copyeditor controls the flow of work to copyeditors and the chief designer (often called art director) controls the flow of the design activity, so the production manager controls the flow of work and materials to printers and binders, and the flow of proofs to and from authors, and the flow of books into the warehouse. The production manager's job, described earlier, is an exceedingly demanding one, since he is the focus of scheduling problems. In a publishing house of any size he will need at least one assistant who mainly looks after schedules, follows up on delays or missed deadlines, makes revised schedules, and informs the various departments of changes so that authors can be notified, advertising rescheduled, and so forth. A good production manager will be alert to problems outside his department—a difficult author, a book-club release date, a major advertising or selling campaign—and will go to great lengths to hold schedules; on the other hand, authors will be late with proofs (often with very good reason), editors or designers may be ill so that proof handling is delayed, and so forth. Such delays (hardly anything ever happens *ahead* of schedule) cause enormous complications in the scheduling of flow through the various stages of printing. Eventually trucks will deliver to the warehouse the hundreds of thousands of books that the house will publish and hopes to sell during the year.

FLOWS AND DECISIONS IN THE MARKETING DEPARTMENT

The marketing department is the outlet for the flow of books that the house is publishing. As we have seen, when the publishing house is viewed as a matching device between authors and readers, the marketing department's function is to connect with the readers. This means that the marketing department must know the individual books that it is selling in order to get them to the individual readers who want them. For most books there is a fairly definable prospective readership—a book on fishing must be sold to fishermen—though there is a large class of books, especially novels, that are sold to "the general reading public," which means essentially the well-educated upper-middle class. Thus even "the general reading public" can be identified as a market, and if it cannot be specified intellectually or occupationally, it can at least be located geographically: urban and suburban concentrated in areas around and between Washington and Boston, around and between New York and Chicago, around and between Seattle and Los Angeles, and around a few major cities elsewhere.

Each book has its market, and we have already said that publishing is "different" because each book is a new enterprise. But books can be grouped according to their markets, and this is the basis of specialization among publishers. Thus a publisher of professional books specializes in reaching the markets for medical, scientific, technical, and business books. He has established channels for the flow of these books and channels for the flow of information to the professionals who want books of this kind and to the specialized libraries such as those maintained by business and industry. He can group these books in advertising and promotion, and he has enough new books to justify special sales efforts directed to these markets. Because he specializes in this market, he will be able to sell more copies of a specialized professional book than another publisher would. The same can be said of other specialties: religious books, juveniles, books of advanced scholarly research, textbooks (specialized at different educational levels), subscription books, encyclopedias, and so forth. Even the publisher of adult trade books is a specialist; he specializes in reaching the "general reader."

Wherever the readers are, the marketing department must inform them about the books that are appropriate and must arrange to make them conveniently available through bookstores and libraries or by mail. The books must flow mainly through the book trade, and to achieve this flow the marketing department must inform the book trade by advertising and direct selling to bookstores. Thus the efforts of the marketing department are split into two areas: informing prospective readers and informing the book trade. Except for displaying books in the stores and some modest cooperative advertising partly paid for by publishers, most bookstores do little to attract readers. Therefore the marketing department will have an advertising program directed mainly to readers and a sales program directed almost exclusively to the trade, including wholesalers.

The mention of wholesalers introduces other important markets which are difficult to classify as "readers," namely, libraries and government, including school systems and school libraries. Libraries buy most of their books through wholesalers, as does the federal government. School systems buy textbooks directly from publishers and library books through wholesalers. In every case purchasers must be informed by the publishers, and in the case of school textbooks, where course adoptions mean large sales, very special and extensive efforts are made, including holding conferences for teachers, showing specially prepared films, distributing many complimentary copies, and so forth.

Still another important and especially interesting area is foreign sales. England has long been a market for American books, and since World War II, with the emergence of English as the world language for science, engineering, and medicine, American books in those fields have been in demand everywhere. Moreover, with the emergence of the United States as a world super-power, the distribution of all kinds of American books has assumed importance, partly through government programs such as those of the U.S. Information Service and the Agency for International Development and partly through the general expansion of interest in and awareness of the United States.

The foreign educational market, too, has an interest for

American publishers, though it has been rare for a foreign country to use an American textbook in English. (This is changing. American textbooks are increasingly used, especially at college and postgraduate levels, and especially in countries like the Netherlands and Denmark, where all educated people speak English and where there is a relatively small literature or book market in the local language.) But there is great interest in American educational methods; there are rights to be sold, and some American publishers are affiliating with foreign publishers or publishing their own adapted foreign-language editions (e.g., in Spanish for the Latin American market). Special low-priced editions are also published in Japan, Korea, India, and other Asian countries, partly to get ahead of the book pirates in Taiwan and elsewhere, and partly to meet special needs in underdeveloped countries with little foreign currency.

A fascinating aspect of foreign sales is its relation to international affairs. The fortunes of the American book abroad go up or down as the international monetary situation fluctuates and as American policy changes. A marketing manager in charge of foreign sales will follow international affairs and U.S. government programs closely, and he will travel and maintain direct contact with booksellers and others in many parts of the world.

To achieve this flow of information from the publishing house to prospective readers and to the book trade at home and abroad, there is a regular cycle of work in the marketing department: a semiannual sales conference at which editors describe new books to salesmen, preparation of a semiannual direct mail and space advertising program, scheduled selling trips to bookstores, college campuses, and school districts, periodic calls on various government agencies, preparation of publicity programs for the printed media and for television and radio, special information for libraries, arrangements to exhibit books at appropriate conventions, distribution of special catalogues for foreign countries, exhibits at international book fairs, and so forth.

And the flow comes full circle in one aspect of the marketing department's activity, namely, the advertising that is intended to impress the name of the publishing house on present and prospective authors. This is a very important aspect of some of the most flamboyant and expensive advertising in the general media such as the book-review sections of metropolitan newspapers. It is also an important aspect of arrangements for author appearances on television and radio programs and at autographing parties in bookstores. An author likes to see his book advertised, whether or not a particular advertisement is truly efficient in terms of sales. Authors tend to bring their manuscripts to publishers who advertise their books effectively or, better yet, lavishly. So a part of the marketing department's activity, while seeming to be aimed at selling books, is really intended to impress authors—and, of course, one hopes that such advertisements will sell books too.

Finally, all this flow of information from the marketing department to the book trade and to readers, and all this flow of work within the marketing department itself, is not constant. The stream bed, so to speak, is constantly changing as new and different books are published and as the markets themselves change —owing to changes in public taste, in educational methods, in government support for various kinds of programs (educational, libraries, slum rehabilitation, etc.), in the distribution and educational level of populations; the growth and movement of industry; the expansion of universities; changes in the international situation; and so forth. For these reasons the marketing department is one of the most dynamic and interesting areas of publishing.

SCHEDULING

Scheduling the flow of work on an individual book is technically simple because the stages of production are a step-by-step sequence from manuscript through galley and page proofs to bound books, so the more complex techniques of production scheduling are not applicable. Nevertheless scheduling is one of the most vexing problems in publishing because of the uncertainties in parts of the schedule, especially in those parts involving the author (mainly reading proof), who is outside the control of the management. When a printer gives a cost estimate, he usually also provides a production schedule based on a certain date for beginning composition, or he is asked for a schedule to produce finished books by a certain date. Such schedules allow intervals for galley and page-proof reading by the author (as well as whatever time is needed by the editor and designer in the house), and these intervals are usually specified by the production manager on the basis of experience plus knowledge obtained from the editor (Is the author going to be able to read proofs immediately? How long does he expect to take? Is he reliable?).

Most printers keep to their schedules reasonably well *if the proofs are returned on time*, but if proofs are late the printer's internal scheduling is thrown off and the book may be greatly delayed. This causes problems with the author, who cannot understand why his book should be delayed a month because he was three days late with his proofs; and it causes problems in the advertising department and elsewhere. So it is important to make schedules that *from the beginning* are realistic and practicable, based on careful estimates of times required for proof stages, including time for mailing to and from the author and time for editorial and design work in the house. Here there is no substitute for direct discussion with the author, emphasizing the importance of keeping to a schedule and pointing out the probable delay from a broken schedule.

However, even if the author performs on schedule—and authors vary greatly in this regard—the editor and designer who must handle the proof in the house often do not allow enough time for their work, or for internal routing. Thus the author's and editor's estimates of time needed should be checked against experience, and it is well for the production manager (or a scheduler on his staff) to keep and compile records showing times needed for the various stages of many books. From these records per-page averages can be worked out for some kinds of work, especially copyediting and proofreading, and reasonable estimates can be made for each stage on the basis of experience.

A basic difficulty is that every book, with few exceptions, is in a hurry. Once the author has finished writing it, he wants it published immediately, regardless of whether it is actually timely—indeed he may have spent ten years writing it. Staff members too, particularly editors, become committed to books and want to push them through quickly, and this is all to the good. In general, the more quickly and smoothly a book goes through production, the less it will cost. Delays cause and provide opportunities for expensive revisions in proof. But not every book can be on an express schedule, and fast schedules are more likely to be broken. Priorities must be set, and the number of express schedules must be kept within reason, perhaps five percent of the total.

Whatever type of schedule is used, some books will be more rushed than others, either because they are more timely or in response to pressure from important authors. A timely book, one that must be ready for the Christmas trade or for a book-club selection or for the school year, must often be scheduled backward. That is, one starts from the desired publication date and works backward to the present, allowing time as necessary for the various stages. Sometimes this causes problems and requires shortcuts; for example, the author and editor may go to the printer's to check proof as it is ready and send it back into production piecemeal. Such shortcuts are dangerous but sometimes necessary; under rushed schedules errors are easily made, and corrections are either expensive or time-consuming or impossible. Quality can easily be sacrificed in a rush schedule, and this must be avoided. The best schedule is one that does not put too much pressure on any of the people who must work on the book in its various stages, but keeps the book moving so that time is not wasted.

In the preceding sections we have mentioned the importance of scheduling the work in each department, and this is of course a responsibility of the department head. The chief copyeditor must know what manuscripts are coming in, how long they are, what editorial complications are anticipated, and what the schedule requirements are. This information must be placed against a knowledge of the work load and capabilities of each copyeditor. Thus the flow of editorial work is controlled in detail. Much the same is true in the design department, though the chief designer has a little more time to plan because he knows from the editorial department and from the production schedule when work on each individual book will be needed. As we have already seen, the marketing department works mainly on a seasonal schedule so far as sales are concerned, but the advertising of each book must be timed to correspond to its scheduled date of publication.

We have discussed the work as if all of it were being done by staff members in the publishing house, but most houses use freelance copyeditors and designers at least occasionally. This has important advantages in scheduling, since freelancers can be called on to ease overloads on the staff and keep the work moving. Its disadvantages are that it reduces the management's control of the work, particularly with regard to quality, and in any case the freelancer cannot know the internal methods or approaches or styles of the house, and he is not as easily available in the house for consultation and conferences with the author, marketing department, or others. If freelancers are used, a staff member must act as liaison to supervise their work and provide the necessary communication that would otherwise take place in the normal course of internal activity. This supervision can be a time-consuming and difficult job, and its cost must be included when considering the relative advantages of freelance versus regular staff. Nevertheless, freelance help is often useful in planning and maintaining schedules during overload periods.

At this point it may be illuminating to outline the flow of work through the editorial, design, production, marketing, and accounting departments. It will be seen that a book does not simply progress from department to department; it passes back and forth at various stages through the departments, the first three being concerned mainly with the production of the book and marketing and accounting being concerned with distribution. Chart I (page 80) shows the variety of activities that typically take place as a book progresses through various stages. This chart was prepared by Ezra S. Diman at the University of Wisconsin Press, and a few aspects would be different (timing of sales activity, concern about special type or "sorts") for a general publisher.

In general, schedules require constant attention, and all staff members must be conscious of them. Changes in schedules must be quickly noted, adjustments must be made, and revised information distributed. The publisher in a house of any size will not be able to watch individual schedules; he must set up procedures and rely on staff members to do this. The publisher will, however, watch the overall rate of production and will take particular note of the schedules of important books. He will review the schedules with department heads and he may take action on schedules if a conflict arises, perhaps giving priority to one book over another. But his main concerns must be the flow of input of manuscripts and output of published books, not the details of scheduling, because the flow of input determines the future output and because the output is very quickly reflected in sales results, which appear on the operating statement and affect the balance sheet. The continuing operating expenses of the house require a steady output at a certain level of books per year or per month, and a slowing of schedules (or an acceleration) produces changes in cash requirements and in profit that must be anticipated. Thus a discussion of schedules leads directly to a consideration of financial aspects of publishing.

FINANCIAL PLANNING

The remainder of this chapter deals with the financial management of a publishing house, a difficult technical subject which cannot be treated thoroughly in the compass of this book. There are many excellent textbooks on accounting and financial management. Here, with particular reference to publishing, we shall briefly discuss the basic financial reports: the balance sheet, operating statement, and cash-flow analysis. These three interrelated documents can tell the publisher what has happened in the past and where matters stand at the moment, but by themselves they cannot tell him what is likely to happen. And it is important to remember that decisions are always made for the future; the past is over and done with—you start from where you are. But you must know where you are, and the balance sheet shows that. And you must learn from your past; the operating statement shows that. And you must use your present cash to generate future cash; the cash-flow analysis shows how money flows through the system, being converted first into assets and then back into money.

So these three reports are primarily useful as a means of molding and predicting the future. The experience and knowledge that they represent must be used as the basis for decisions that will determine the future, and the financial plan for the future is called the budget. The budget should be thought of as a set of realizable goals. Budgets, by allocating funds to divisions or departments of a publishing house, are useful as a means of control, and because of this they may be thought of as restrictions. But a wise publisher will regard his budget not as a restriction but a plan, and he will change his plan as circumstances develop, spending his money where he thinks it will have the best future effect. We shall discuss budgeting for long-range effects in the chapter on planning; here we are more concerned with short-term effects.

The principal budget, called the operating budget, is usually a projection of the operating statement for the year ahead. It is equally important, however, to project the flow of cash into the future, envisioning the conversion of cash into inventories and other assets and anticipating the income that will be generated—to be sure that there will be enough cash when it is needed. And this leads to a projection of a future balance sheet, that is, a picture of the house's probable future financial condition.

In Chapter II we described the accounting department as a service group, touching all other departments and providing the management with financial and other information necessary to permit it to control operations. The three basic financial reports—balance sheet, operating statement, and cash-flow analysis—are the means of doing this; and their projections into the future, called the budget, express the financial aspect of the overall plan for the future of the house.

The Balance Sheet

The balance sheet is a snapshot of the financial condition of the house at a given time, so a sequence of balance sheets over a period of time will provide a kind of time-lapse movie of the house's fortunes. Examination of any one balance sheet may show whether the house is in good or poor financial health, but by itself it will not show the direction of movement, although usually a balance sheet shows at least two years, so it is possible to observe changes. The balance sheet, together with the operating statement, discussed below, shows both the house's state of health and its direction of progress. And both can be better understood against a background of knowledge of micro-publishing activity.

A typical balance sheet would include the following items:

ASSETS

Current Assets
- Cash and marketable securities
- Bank certificates and government securities
- Accounts receivable less estimated losses on collection
- Inventories less reserve against write-off

Royalty Advances to Authors

Fixed Assets
- Land
- Buildings
- Furniture and fixtures
- Equipment
- Leasehold improvements
- Miscellaneous (long-term investments, cash value of life insurance, etc.)

LIABILITIES

Current Liabilities
- Accounts payable
- Accrued payroll
- Notes payable to banks
- Royalties payable
- Advance payments
- Reserves for taxes
- Dividends declared but not paid
- Reserves for contingencies

Long-Term Liabilities
- Mortgages
- Bonds and other long-term payables
- Reserves for depreciation
- Preferred stock
- Common stock
- Retained earnings (surplus)

The difference between the current assets and the current liabilities is the net working capital available to run the publishing activity on a day-to-day basis. This is a figure that must be watched and related to other factors such as inventories, short-term debts, and so forth. A common general measure of the financial health of a business is the ratio of current assets to current liabilities, often called the "current ratio," and the business is said to be healthy if the current ratio exceeds two to one. This is of course only a generality based on one specific ratio which changes day to day, and so one must look at other aspects of the balance sheet to understand the real situation.

For example, the proportion of inventories in the current assets is important, particularly in relation to short-term debts. If too much of the current assets are tied up in slow-moving inventories, it may not be possible to make scheduled payments on short-term debts. To examine this aspect the so-called "quick ratio" is useful; this is the ratio of liquid assets (current assets less inventories and other items not immediately convertible to cash) to short-term debts. A "quick ratio" of one to one is reassuring. If it is less than one to one, an examination of inventory turnover (ratio of annual sales to inventories) is immediately in order, to see how quickly the inventories are likely to be turned into cash. And this immediately leads to the question of the aging of receivables: How long after a book is sold, on the average, is it paid for? This can be examined by a month by month analysis of receivables, which the accounting department should prepare in the normal process of credit control; but a quick estimate can be made by comparing the total receivables to the total annual sales.

One can easily see that the interpretation of the balance sheet depends on an understanding of what is going on in the publishing house, and for this reason it is difficult to assign standard ratios such as two to one for the "current ratio" and one to one for the "quick ratio." It is noteworthy that while one wants to keep thc ratio of current assets to current liabilities as high as possible, one also wants to keep the current assets as low as possible, in order to minimize the investment required to maintain a certain volume of business. The situation must be judged in relation to the past experience of the house, the direction of change, the type of publishing, and the industry experience. For example, educational publishers need to maintain relatively larger inventories than adult trade publishers. Collections of receivables from school systems and government agencies tend to be slow. Both these factors make heavy demands on the working capital of educational publishers.

All this has to do with the short-term health of the house, but one must also keep in mind the long-term situation. What is the relationship of the working capital to the long-term debt? If the long-term debt should exceed the working capital, it would mean that the house was currently operating completely on borrowed funds, and interest payments might prove too heavy a burden. Another comparison might be made between fixed assets and net worth; if the fixed assets exceed three-fourths of the net worth, perhaps too much of the house's capital is tied up in fixed assets. This would be rare in a publishing house, but some of the larger houses have recently invested heavily in real estate and buildings.

Although there is no substitute for careful analysis and projection of what is actually happening in a publishing house, the following rough indicators may be helpful:

Ratio	*Index*
current assets: current liabilities	at least 2:1
liquid assets: short-term debt	at least 1:1
annual net sales: inventories	at least 2.5:1
working capital: inventories	at least 1.3:1
annual net sales: receivables	at least 3:1

These indicators can be used as bench marks or danger signals; to know what they mean, one must go behind them to see what is happening and in what direction change is progressing. What changes have taken place in the past year or in the past several years? How have inventories changed in relation to sales? Has the long-term debt increased or decreased, and how does it relate to working capital? What has been the change in fixed assets? And so forth.

In discussing the ratios that may guide the publisher in his financial management, we must remember that the owners or shareholders are interested in another ratio, namely, the ratio of profit to investment. The owners expect the publishing house to maintain a certain level of profit, but their actual return on investment will be sharply affected by the capital structure of the house, that is, how much of the assets are financed by funds bearing a limited return (long-term debt, preferred stock, etc.) and how much is payable to the owners on account of their residual equity interest. This effect, called capital structure leverage, will vary greatly from one house to another, so here we can consider only the profitability of the house as a whole. The profitability ratio, or earning power, is the net operating income divided by the operating assets; this is what the profit-oriented publisher tries to maximize. He does this by means of sales, turning over the assets (turnover = sales/assets) to produce a profit margin (= net income/sales), but in the equation

$$\text{Profitability} = \text{asset turnover} \times \text{profit margin} = \frac{\text{net income}}{\text{assets}}$$

sales cancel out. Publishers may become very sales-oriented, and an increase of sales should produce an increase of profit in a well-managed house, but the publisher's financial task is to manage the assets to produce profit, so the ratio of profit to assets is what he must ultimately watch.

The Operating Statement

Another way to see what is happening as time passes is to look at the operating statement, sometimes called the income statement or profit and loss statement. This shows the accumulated results of operations during part or all of the fiscal year, often in relation to the budget for the period. Items included would be income from sales, royalties accrued, accumulated plant cost, production costs of books sold, income from subsidiary rights, and detailed departmental and general operating expenses; these are usually shown as a percentage of sales. Since a house can operate at a good profit and still run out of working capital because of overexpansion, the operating statement must be read with the balance sheet. However, with sound accounting practices, whether the house is showing a profit is immediately apparent from the operating statement, as are the results in relation to expectations as shown by the budget.

A typical publisher's operating statement would contain the items shown in Table II, and a large publishing house would probably have additional operating statements for each of its divisions (juvenile, technical, adult trade, etc.). Typical percentages* for several types of publishers are shown as examples.

* These figures are abstracted and adjusted from summary reports prepared by Ernst & Ernst for the American Book Publishers Council.

The typical operating statement, with percentages for various kinds of publishers, calls for some comment. At the bottom of the statement the low percentages of net income after taxes show that publishing is not a highly profitable business on the average, though some publishers do much better than the average, and one highly successful textbook or best seller can make an enormous difference. In general one is struck more by the similarities in the percentage columns than by the differences, and most of the differences are readily explained in terms of the characteristics of the particular publishing specialty.

It is not surprising that the returns from bookstores are highest in the adult trade category, since adult trade books require maximum exposure in bookstores during the relatively short period when an intense effort is being made to focus the attention of the public on the book. When a book fails to catch on, a lot of copies must be returned. Likewise it is not surprising that publishers of religious books have the highest production cost and the lowest plant cost; this is because of the effect of Bibles and prayer books on the overall percentages. A Bible, once it has been set in type, is usually printed in a very large number of copies over a long period, and the price will be low in relation to the number of pages and the cost of printing, paper, and binding. The percentage of inventory write-off for university presses appears to be high, perhaps because university publishers are consistently overoptimistic about the sales of their specialized scholarly books, but also because such books sell over long periods of time, and a publisher may want to have enough stock to last ten years but will prudently write off remaining stock after five.

Under operating expenses, one can see noticeable differences, especially in the marketing area, both in total expenditure and in its distribution between selling and promotional activity. As one would expect, adult trade publishers have the highest percentage of total marketing expense (19%) and nearly the highest in each of the two subcategories. The extraordinarily high advertising and promotional expense of university presses (14%) is mainly a re-

TABLE II

Typical operating statement	*Adult trade*	*Juvenile*	*Religious*	*Profes-sional*	*Univer-sity press*
Gross sales	114%	106%	104%	112%	108%
Returns and allowances	14%	6%	4%	12%	8%
Net sales	100%	100%	100%	100%	100%
Less: Cost of books sold					
Production cost (paper, printing, and binding)	32	40	49	32	42*
Plant cost	6	4	3	4	
Royalties and advances written off	16	10	6	12	11
Inventory write-off	2	0.3	2	2	4
Total cost of books sold	56	54.3	60	50	57
Gross profit on sales	44	45.7	40	50	43
Add: Other publishing income (sale of rights, etc.)	8	2.3	1	2	3
Total operating income	52	48	41	52	46
Less: Operating expenses					
Editorial department	4	3	2.5	4	8
Production department (includes design)	2	1	2	2	3

Marketing department:					
Selling expense	7	7	5	8	4
Advertising and promotion expense	12	6	7	9	14
Shipping and warehousing	5	5	4.5	4	5
General and administrative expense	13	12	12	15	21
Total operating expenses	43	34	33	42	55
Net income from operations	9	14	8	10	(9)
Nonpublishing income or expenses	1	0	0	0	0
Net income before state and federal taxes	10	14	8	10	(9)
State and federal taxes	5	7	4	5	0
Net income after taxes	5	7	4	5	(9)†

* This is manufacturing cost before subsidies; specific title subsidies amount to about 6%, producing a manufacturing cost after subsidies of 36%.

( ) indicates negative figure.

† The subsidies applicable to individual titles (6%) reduce the overall loss to 3%, which must be covered by general subsidies provided by university funds or by endowment.

flection of the necessity to do a certain minimum of advertising even for those books that will have very small sales, rather than a tendency to splurge. Similarly, for university presses, the high percentage of general and administrative expense (21%) and the high editorial percentage (8%) reflect the necessity to maintain a basic organizational structure on a small sales base.

From inspection of the typical operating statements, the reader may draw further conclusions on the characteristics of different branches of book publishing. One might note, for example, the extreme importance for adult trade publishers of the sale of book club and other rights; without such income their profits would be low indeed. Or one could look behind the figures presented here to examine the proportion of current to backlist sales in the various types of publishing. One would discover that adult trade publishers netted 57% of their hardback sales from current books and only 43% from the backlist, whereas publishers of juveniles net only 20% from the current list and 80% from the backlist. Obviously adult trade publishing is much less stable than the publication of juveniles.

Average percentages of net sales for items in the operating statement, issued annually by the American Book Publishers Council, the American Educational Publishers Institute, and the Association of American University Presses, are available to members in an operating-ratio report. This is a very carefully prepared document to which a large number of publishers contribute confidential financial reports, based on uniform definitions of terms so as to provide comparable results. It can serve as a helpful guide in preparing a budget or in analyzing current operations. It must always be remembered, however, that the reliability of any operating statement depends on the accuracy of a number of estimates (depreciation, inventory evaluation, etc.), and a careful publisher will make sure that his own accounting practices are sound and will be aware of the current state of the industry generally. He will ask himself: How do the current figures compare with industry averages? How does the budget compare? What are the reasons for the differences? These questions can be asked for every item, and indeed the ratio report gives averages by item so that it would be impossible for any house to be average in every item—the averages do not add up to 100%. That is why the percentages in Table I have been adjusted to be typical rather than average.

The industry averages are a useful measuring rod and should be used for comparison, but departure from the averages is not necessarily an indication of something wrong. The industry average for advertising and promotion expense is 9% for publishers of professional books, but the percentage spent on individual books will vary sharply from book to book. Some books will do well on a small program of simple announcements by direct mail and in professional journals; others may require elaborate campaigns and space in expensive media. The results and the percentages will vary, as the mix of books on a house's list will vary, and the level of advertising expenditure must be a matter for judgment.

The decision on an advertising budget, either for the list as a whole or for an individual book, is an attempt to reach an optimum, the point beyond which additional expenditure will not produce a *commensurate* increase in sales. How much sales in dollars must be produced by each *additional* advertising dollar? The amount will vary from book to book; certainly one wants to recover as a minimum the production cost of the book plus the cost of the advertising plus handling cost.

If the advertising is efficient, sales should rise rapidly as advertising expenditures increase, and then less rapidly as expenditures go beyond a certain point. This is a typical pattern both for an individual book and for the list as a whole. One must concentrate one's attention on *additional* sales per *additional* advertising dollar spent. When this ratio falls to a certain level, additional advertising will not result in enough additional sales to justify the expense.

The problem, of course, is that one rarely knows the exact results of any particular advertising effort. Judgment and experience must be brought to bear in setting the budget, and continuous efforts must be made to relate actual sales to selling and advertising expense. In this regard the industry averages are useful, as are discussions with other publishers concerning their own experiences with individual books. Advertising agencies may be very helpful in getting maximum effect from a particular budget, but they are often not as able as the publisher himself to relate the expenditure to the result, and ultimately it is the publisher who must set the budget.

The Operating Budget

The operating statement, in addition to showing what has happened during a fiscal year, provides the basis for a projection into the future, namely, an operating budget, which will consist of an estimate of what the operating statement will show at the end of the *next* fiscal year and at various times (perhaps quarterly) in between. Making such a budget is a substantial task but it is a therapeutic one, for it forces the publisher to look ahead and it can reveal macro-publishing difficulties at an early stage.

Since the operating budget expresses the financial aspects of the plan of operations for the coming year, it must be developed by the top management of the house, that is, the chief executive officers and the department heads. The particular approach will depend on the nature of the house and the personal preferences of the chief executives. In a large commercial publishing house with several divisions, the management will first be concerned to decide where they want to build for the future in terms of larger investment. What segments of the industry are booming? What segments are having problems? What government programs will affect book sales? What types of publishing are most profitable? How can the firm take best advantage of the opportunities, and which divisions of the company should be strengthened or expanded? Once such decisions are made, budgeting for the divisions can begin, involving the division heads and the principal officers and, directly or indirectly, the department heads of the divisions. Thus the plan for the company is broken down into individual plans, including goals, for the various departments.

A small publishing house may face much the same questions if it considers branching into new areas—for example, juveniles or reference books—but its main budgeting problem will be more like that of a division of a large house, except that it must be entirely self-sufficient. It cannot draw on cash supplied by income from other divisions, its assets and liabilities are not merged into those of a larger entity, and its profit or loss will not be balanced against profits or losses from other activities. Thus a small house is more sensitive to changes in the particular area of its operations, which makes budgeting all the more important. The principal officers and department heads will look carefully at the probable financial effects of publishing schedules, sales and advertising programs, personnel changes, manufacturing plans, and other activities, adjusting where necessary to meet anticipated contingencies. It is important to emphasize that since the budget is a plan, as the year goes by it should be compared with actual results, and if necessary new plans (and a new budget) should be prepared.

Textbooks on financial management describe a variety of forecasting techniques useful for budgeting. Analysis of historical experience is essential—averages and percentages can be applied to future operations—but there is no substitute for detailed knowledge of specific future projects combined with imagination and foresight. Routine application of averages and percentages from past experience can fail to anticipate predictable changes, so budgeting techniques must be adapted to particular situations in individual publishing houses. Nevertheless it may be helpful to examine a possible method of budgeting in a small publishing house, though the following exposition should be regarded as illustrative rather than prescriptive.

To make such a budget, one might begin with the list of books to be published during the coming year, as far as it is known, and with estimates for as yet unknown books to be published toward the end of the year. These books may be taken into precise account in quarterly or semiannual revisions of the budget, when they are known. An estimated publication date, quantity, plant and production cost, price and discount category, and rate of sale are needed for each title. From this information the approximate sales income from newly published books can be calculated. To this sum must be added the estimated sales income from backlist books, calculated from a study of individual titles or by the use of projections based on experience. Thus one can arrive at an estimated total sales income, and total income can be obtained by adding the estimated income from subsidiary rights, based on specific information or previous averages or both.

The manufacturing information on new books leads directly to the budget item for plant cost. To this must be added the plant cost of reprints during the year, which requires a review of backlist books and a projection of reprints and their costs. The total of projected plant costs becomes the budget item in that category.

The production cost of books sold must be developed from the projected sales of new and backlist books, already completed. If the production cost (estimated or actual) of each book is known, one simply takes the sum of production cost times number of copies to be sold of each title; for the backlist, averages can be applied. It should be noted that this is the production cost *in inventory*; if the books have been written off, the production cost for accounting purposes is zero.

Royalties can also be projected by multiplying the number of copies expected to be sold by the royalty in each case.

It should be noted here that, although not explicitly stated in the budget, the budget-making process reveals the number of copies and inventory value of books to be put into inventory during the year and also shows how the inventory will be reduced by the sale of books. The difference between these two items is the change in investment in inventory and will reveal either the availability of more cash for operations or perhaps the need for more working capital to sustain the inventory. If the inventory change is great, especially if it appears to be increasing rapidly, a change in policy of determining quantities of original print orders or reprint orders may be indicated. A reduction of quantities will of course reduce inventory and make cash available; it will also increase the frequency of reprints and raise plant costs slightly. This complex matter should be studied in the light of the discussion in Chapters IV and V.

Returning to the budget, we next look at operating expenses. Here each department head must be consulted about expected activities and costs, and usually the department head is responsible for working within the budget for his department, once it is set. Here is where the micro-publishing activities of each department must fit the framework of macro-publishing. Title expenditures such as advertising must be worked out in detail or made to fit a projected total. Salaries and office overhead are, of course, fairly easy to project.

The "general and administrative" expenses are always a large item, of which the biggest part is the accounting and order-processing department. The overall management (the publisher's office and staff) is usually included here, though it may be shown separately, especially if it is desired to relate accounting-department activity closely to total sales.

The result of this totaling of incomes and expenses is a projected profit or loss. If the profit is unsatisfactory or (for a nonprofit publisher) the loss too great, the budget must be re-examined to see whether adjustments in budget items, which mean changes in activity, can produce a better result. In fact *any* budget, once it has been completed by developing the budgets of the different departments and forecasting sales and other results, should be carefully examined to see whether its parts are in balance and whether it can be improved. The advertising budget may be cut—or it may be increased to try for more sales. Editorial travel may be increased or decreased, to get more better-selling books or to save money. Personnel changes may be made. And so forth. In short, the budget is used not only as a projection but also as a means of planning in order to get a desired result, and in order to foresee problems before they become acute.

*Cash-Flow Analysis and Projection**

One might think at first that the balance sheet and operating statement together would tell a publisher all he needed to know about the financial health of his house. But there is a prosaic but sometimes embarrassing problem that can arise to plague a publisher who is satisfied with a sound balance sheet and a profitable operation—the problem of cash. Accrual accounting can conceal the flow of cash in its recording of various noncash transactions, and not only paper profits but actual money will be needed to meet payrolls, to pay royalties and printers' bills, and to provide for interest payments and dividends to stockholders, for example. Profits that are tied up in inventories or receivables are not much help when the bills come due, except perhaps as collateral for a loan. In a publishing house operated for a profit, the people who put cash into it expect to get cash out eventually. And even a nonprofit house needs cash for all publishing expenses, except dividends.

A cash-flow analysis shows where money came from and what it was used for. It connects two balance sheets by means of the operating statement that covers the period between them. It shows how the profit, noncash items, expenses, and sources of cash interact to lead from the beginning supply of cash to the cash on hand at the end of the period.

A historical cash-flow analysis is sometimes labeled "Sources and Uses of Funds," usually covering a year or a year to date. The form of the report can be seen in the following example.

* For an excellent discussion of this subject from a general point of view, see "Cash Flow Analysis for Managerial Control," *Research Report No. 38* of the National Association of Accountants, 1961. The following discussion draws heavily on this report.

SOURCES AND USES OF FUNDS
YEAR ENDED DECEMBER 31, 19__

Sources of Funds	
Net income before taxes	$420,000
Noncash charges to operations (depreciation, write-offs, provision for deferred income taxes, etc.)	280,000
Changes in liability accounts (other than bank loans)	(35,000)
Funds generated by operations	$665,000
Bank loans	57,000
Captial stock issued	230,000
Total funds available	$952,000
Uses of Funds	
Acquisition, construction, and replacement of property and equipment	486,000
Income taxes	115,000
Dividends	163,000
Investments	15,000
Interest payments and reduction of long-term debt	42,000
Increase (decrease) in accounts receivable	(13,000)
Increase (decrease) in inventories	33,000
Advance royalties and prepaid expenses	24,000
Total funds used	$865,000
Increase (decrease) in cash and marketable securities	87,000
Cash and marketable securities, beginning of period	312,000
Cash and marketable securities, end of period	399,000

As can be seen, this report works backward from the net income or profit, adding the noncash expenses such as depreciation and cash supplied from outside sources. The cash expenditures are then subtracted, providing a figure for the net change in cash and marketable securities, which can be added to (or subtracted from) the starting figure.

In the same way, once the operating budget has been prepared, the "Sources and Uses of Funds" format can be used to predict the cash available at the end of the budgeted period. One simply starts with the budgeted net income and works backward in the same way, adding and subtracting anticipated cash income and expenditures. It should be pointed out that this method is not exact because of the effect of internal accounting transactions that have no corresponding cash flows (e.g., changes in the valuation of inventories), but it is normally satisfactory for planning purposes. The manager must be sure to have enough cash on hand to meet needs, but since cash can be profitably invested, it is desirable not to keep more on hand than necessary.

This formal cash-flow analysis and projection should provide confidence that enough cash will be available to maintain the publishing activity—or it will reveal the need for additional financing or the possibility of short-term investing. It will not, however, relieve the accounting department and its manager of the problem of watching the day-to-day matters that affect the supply of cash: the amount, structure, and aging of receivables; the amount of work in process; the need to meet payrolls and current bills; and the like. Fluctuations within the budgeted period can make problems in these areas, though the formal report should provide confidence that such problems can be handled by short-term arrangements if necessary.

In all, the balance sheet and operating statement, along with the budget and cash-flow projection, are used to observe the flow of activity and make a sequence of decisions at the macro-publishing level. Macro-publishing situations control the micro-publishing activity, and micro-publishing activity largely creates the macro-publishing situations. The micro-publishing activity develops from a sequence of decisions about individual books (or projects) and the resulting macro-publishing situation requires other decisions that reflect back into the micro-publishing activity. Thus there is a constant interplay between macro-publishing and micro-publishing. It is now time to look in more detail at the quantitative aspects of the micro-publishing activity.

IV

THE ECONOMICS OF MICRO-PUBLISHING

In chapter III we concentrated mainly on the financial aspects of the publishing house as a whole; here we shall look in detail at the economics of publication of an individual book, with particular attention to the determination of the print order, the price, the discount, the royalty rate, and the budget for operating costs related to the book. We shall consider the estimated profit or loss from the publication of a book; and having analyzed these factors, we shall develop an approach to a "publication plan" which takes them into account. The publication plan for an individual book is the synthesis of the publisher's decisions with respect to that book.

In this discussion of the economics of micro-publishing, we shall first consider the relationships and parameters that are involved in setting the prices and print orders of new books and reprints.

A small amount of elementary mathematics is used, but this should not be allowed to give a false impression of precision in an area where judgment is essential and estimates are necessarily imprecise. Nevertheless a careful examination of relationships should be helpful in exercising judgment. A thorough formulation of a problem will at least indicate what factors should be considered by the person exercising judgment, and it may indicate ways in which quantitative experience can be applied in making new decisions.

The logic of this exploration has demanded presentation in what may seem to be reverse order. The question of determining the optimum quantity to print is considered before discussing *whether* a printing will result in a profit or a loss, and reprintings (being simpler) are considered before original printings of new books or new editions. Lastly, we will discuss discounts and royalties.

DETERMINING THE QUANTITY TO PRINT

To arrive at a complete publication plan, we must first consider particular aspects of it, and it will be well to begin with the categories of cost that will have to be taken into account, as follows:

1. Costs incurred up to the time the presses begin to turn
   a. Editorial costs, including cost of search and consideration
   b. Design costs
   c. Production costs of securing estimates and choosing a printer
   d. General overhead costs associated with *a*, *b*, and *c*
   e. Plant costs (typesetting, cost of plates, all manufacturing costs up to the point when the presses begin to roll)
2. Costs incurred after the presses begin to turn
   f. Production costs (presswork, paper, and binding)
   g. Selling costs
   h. Storage costs
   i. Interest on value of inventory*
   j. General overhead costs associated with *f*, *g*, and *h*

* This is a cost because the money invested in inventory, where it does not draw interest, could have been invested at interest. Or perhaps the publisher had to borrow working capital and is actually paying interest.

Assuming that paper is available, the decision on the quantity to print or reprint can be made at the point when the presses begin to turn; in fact, earlier decisions on quantity are often reviewed and adjusted in the light of the latest market information at this time. And by this time all the expenditures under 1 have been made; they are dead and in the past, and they cannot affect the decision for the future, which must depend on the items under 2. Of course the estimated expenditures under 1 were taken into account when deciding *whether* to proceed with a new book or reprint; they are an essential part of the total cost, but they cannot affect the decision on the *quantity* to print or reprint.

The decision on quantity must be made because books are produced in batches, called printings—first printing, second printing, and so forth. This is a requirement of current technology; it is just not economical to do otherwise. Some day we may be able to produce books one at a time, as ordered, so that each day's orders can be manufactured that day and shipped the next. This possible development, to be discussed in a later chapter, would be ideal, since it would avoid the problem of the decision on quantity, with the ensuing problems of storage, interest on inventory investment, and the danger of over- or underprinting. But today's printing technology does not permit one-at-a-time production (except for certain out-of-print books at low quality and high cost), so we are stuck with the problem of determining the batch size, the number of copies to be printed at one time.

Fortunately the problem of determining the most economical batch size was long ago worked out for general application in industrial management. A little reflection will confirm that when the cost of holding a book in inventory exceeds the cost of replacing that book with a newly printed one, that book has been held too long. That is, it is economical to print enough books to last only up to the time when the cost of holding them equals the cost of replacing them. Thus the optimum quantity to produce in any printing will be determined by (*a*) the carrying charges and (*b*) the cost of getting ready to produce the next printing. The carrying charges will of course depend partly on the production cost (*not* the plant cost) of the printing, since this is the value of the inventory against which interest will be charged.

To repeat, *the most economical print order has been determined when the cost of carrying the book in stock exactly equals the plant cost of reprinting it.*

Suppose the unit production cost of a book is \$0.60. If the cost of carrying the book in inventory is 10% per year, at the end of a year its cost is \$0.66; at the end of two years its cost is \$0.726, and so forth. The formula for its accumulated cost is $p \times 1.10^y$, where p = production cost and y = years. But of course (ignoring inflation), if it weren't for the plant cost of reprinting, the book could be reproduced at any time for \$0.60. It is the plant cost of reprinting that prevents one-at-a-time production and the elimination of carrying charges.

The plant cost of reprinting an edition is not difficult to estimate (for this purpose, the office cost of making the decision and ordering the reprinting should be included). Let us call the plant cost R. The percentage cost of carrying charges is more difficult; it depends on several items such as interest on investment in inventory (production cost of inventory only, as already explained), cost of warehousing, loss due to pilferage and damage, etc. Each publishing house must determine its own rate. Of course the carrying charges for a book in inventory during any given year must be calculated only on the actual inventory during that year, not on the starting inventory.

For a book that is selling at a steady rate r, the cost of carrying inventory for y years is

$$\frac{Npcy}{2} \qquad (1)$$

where N = number of copies in beginning inventory
p = unit production cost (excluding plant cost)
c = annual percentage carrying charge
y = years to sell out the edition at rate r
r = annual rate of sale ($ry = N$)

The 2 appears in the denominator because the average inventory during the life of the book is the beginning inventory (N) plus the final inventory (zero) divided by 2. Substituting N/r for y and setting the carrying charges equal to the plant cost of reprinting, we get

$$R = \frac{pcN_{opt}^2}{2r} \tag{2}$$

where N_{opt} is the optimum quantity to print. Solving for N_{opt} gives

$$N_{opt} = \sqrt{\frac{2Rr}{pc}} \tag{3}$$

Let us take an example* in which

R = \$400 plant cost of *next* printing (offset negatives and plates)
p = \$.60 per copy
r = 3000 copies per year
c = 10% per year cost of carrying inventory

$$N_{opt} = \sqrt{\frac{2 \times 400 \times 3000}{0.6 \times 0.1}} = 6300 \text{ copies}$$

If fewer than 6300 copies were ordered, the plant cost of reprinting would occur sooner than necessary and would result in unnecessary cost. If more than 6300 copies were ordered, accumulated carrying charges would cause the cost of the copies beyond 6300 to exceed the replacement cost, and it would have been cheaper to do a new printing. That is, if more than 6300 copies are printed, the copies beyond 6300, by the time they are sold, will cost more than the cost of replacing them with a new printing.

A more general illustration of the determination of the opti-

* Here and in later examples solutions are worked out to slide-rule accuracy and rounded. There is not much point in working out exact solutions when they depend on approximate figures such as estimated future rates of sale. A slide rule or desk calculator will enable a publisher to solve the problems considered here quickly and easily. Also, a print order is likely to be rounded at least to the nearest 100 copies, or to the nearest 500 or 1000 copies.

mum number to reprint is given in Figure 9, which graphs N_{opt} against R for several values of p, assuming that $r = 1000$ copies per year and $c = 10\%$ per year. Figure 9 can even be used for rough graphical solutions. The values above the dotted line would not normally be applicable because most publishers would not want to risk a reprinting for more than three years, and many have maximum reprint cycles of two years or even less.

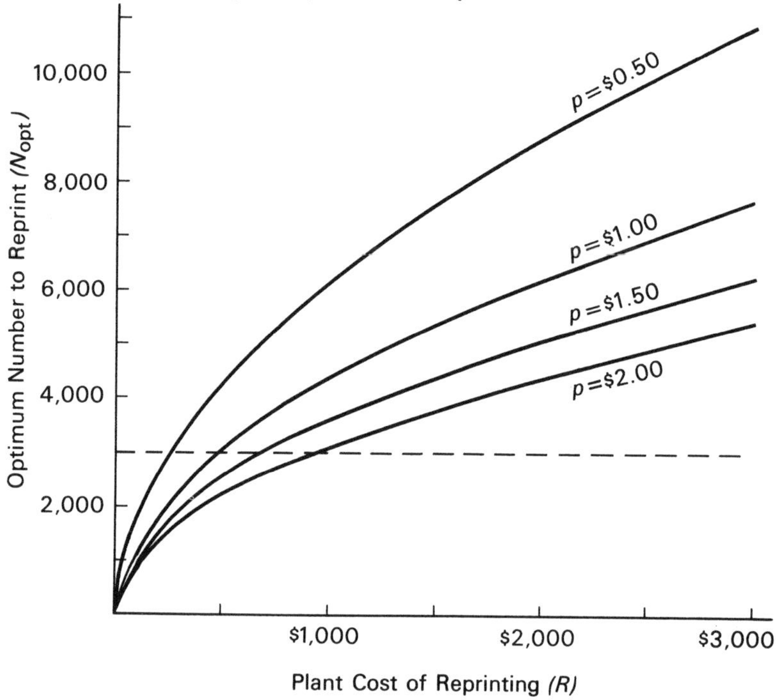

Figure 9

It is important to note that we have treated the unit production cost p as a fixed quantity for any given book. It is the sum of the costs of paper, press time, and binding a single book; of course it will depend on the length of the book and materials used, but once these are established, p is a constant within the range of practical decision-making. There will be a slight change in p if one shifts, let us say, from a sheet-fed to a web press, or from a medium-size to a large press, but such manufacturing decisions can be assumed to be made on the basis of efficiency for the probable length of run, and the decision on the number to print (or reprint) will normally fall well within the range of a particular printing press.

Another factor which gives the illusion of a variable p is the method by which binders normally quote prices. Printers are accustomed to separating plant costs from production costs in billing publishers, but binders normally quote and bill on the basis of complex schedules giving unit binding prices for varying quantities, depending on the type of binding, materials used, etc. The *plant cost of binding*, or setup cost, is built into these schedules, which are used by estimators, and most binders would not easily comply with a publisher's request to separate plant costs from production costs in estimating and billing. It is rather simple, however, if one has the binder's estimate or schedule for the cost of binding 2000 and 5000 copies, for example, to determine the true production cost of binding. Thus if the price for binding 2000 copies is \$1000 and for 5000 copies the price is \$2250, the cost for the additional 3000 copies is \$1250, so the unit production cost of binding must be \$1250 divided by 3000, or \$0.417. The plant cost of binding is therefore the price quoted minus the production cost (\$1000 minus 2000 × \$0.417) or \$166.

In short, the unit production cost p may be regarded as a fixed amount for any particular book, once the design is settled, within the range of practical decisions. In general, it is not true that the unit production cost goes down as quantity increases, in spite of widespread impressions to the contrary; this mistaken idea is caused by the spreading of plant costs, giving a lower *total* unit cost, and this, as we shall see (footnote, page 134), can lead to faulty decisions.

NEW BOOKS

We have applied the formula $N_{opt} = \sqrt{2rR/pc}$ to the problem of a book that is selling at a steady rate and must be reprinted. This is the simplest case, but the reasoning behind the formula will apply equally well to a first printing or to a reprinting for which the rate of sale is not steady, if one substitutes a variable *r* for the constant *r* that has been used so far. It may be found, for example, that sales tend to decline by 50% per year; that is, if 3000 copies are sold in the first year, 1500 will be sold in the second year, 750 in the third, and so on. It will be more convenient to solve this problem graphically, though computers are beginning to help publishers with such problems.

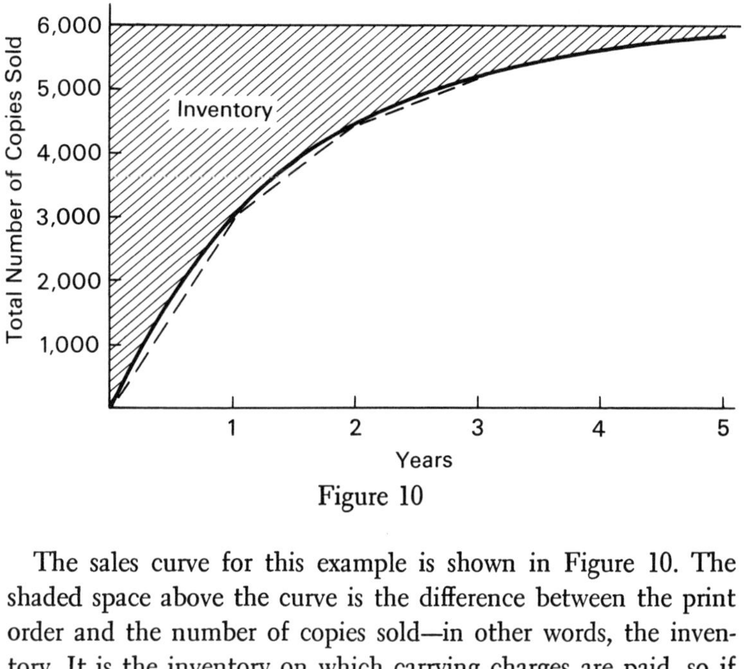

Figure 10

The sales curve for this example is shown in Figure 10. The shaded space above the curve is the difference between the print order and the number of copies sold—in other words, the inventory. It is the inventory on which carrying charges are paid, so if one assumes a print order (6000 copies is assumed in Figure 10), one can calculate the accumulating carrying charges. For this purpose it is simpler and is sufficiently accurate (at least as accurate as the sales forecast) to use a straight-line approximation for the sales curve, as shown by the dotted line. Thus the average inventory during the first year was the print order minus 1500 copies,

TABLE I

			Print 6000 copies			*Print 5500 copies*			*Print 5000 copies*		
Year	Yearly sale (copies)	Total sale (copies)	Average inventory (copies)	Yearly carrying charges	Total carrying charges	Average inventory (copies)	Yearly carrying charges	Total carrying charges	Average inventory (copies)	Yearly carrying charges	Total carrying charges
1st	3000	3000	4500	270	270	4000	240	240	3500	210	210
2nd	1500	4500	2250	135	405	1750	105	345	1250	75	285
3rd	750	5250	1125	67.5	472.50	625	38	383	125	7.50	292.50
4th	375	5625	562	33.75	506.25	62	4	387			
5th	188	5813	281	16.87	523.12						

for the second year it was the print order minus 3750 copies, for the third year it was the print order minus 4875 copies, and so on.

Remembering that the carrying charges are Npc, we can construct Table I, assuming several different possible print orders.

From Table I we can plot the total carrying charges for each of the several possible printings, as shown in Figure 11. The intersection of that line with the line indicating the plant cost of reprinting gives the optimum number N to print.

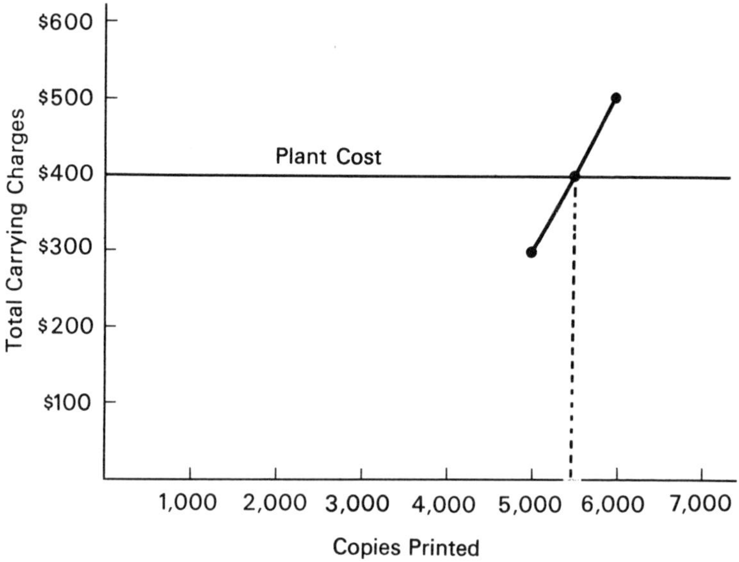

Figure 11

The optimum printing in the example is approximately 5500 copies, within the range of accuracy of the sales forecast. A printing of this size (plus the allowance for free and review copies) should be ordered.

The same argument, and formula, can be used to determine the optimum quantity to bind and rebind, since bindings are made in batches like printings. In this case R = the setup cost for a rebinding; p = the unit cost of binding; and c and r are the same as before. If the formula is to be used to determine binding quantities of an edition, it should be applied only to the sheets (without binding) to determine the print order of that edition. In that case p is the unit production cost of sheets; the other parameters remain the same.

SENSITIVITY

Even if the formula $N_{opt} = \sqrt{2Rr/pc}$ is theoretically correct, how useful is it? One can never determine the values of R, r, p, and c exactly; how much difference will it make if some of these values are incorrect?

First, it is important to emphasize again that the formula is a guide to judgment. The publisher will want to estimate in each case whether sales will continue at a steady rate, whether a book will become outdated, and so forth. Even so, how accurately must R, r, p, and c be determined?

It is evident from the formula that N_{opt} is proportional to $\sqrt{R}$ and $\sqrt{r}$; or

$$N_{opt} = K_1 \sqrt{R}; \quad N_{opt} = K_2 \sqrt{r}$$

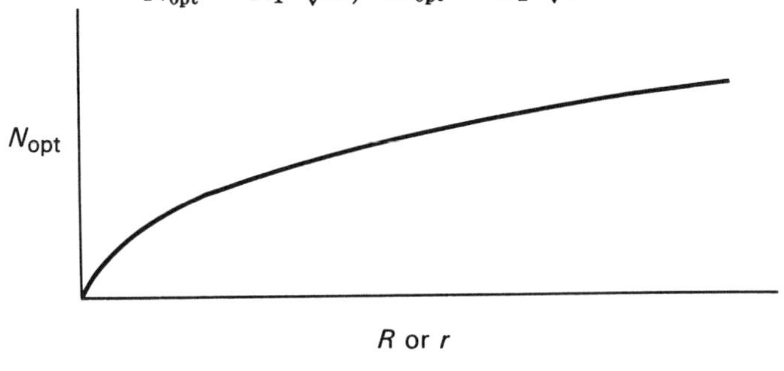

Figure 12

If R or r doubles, N increases by a factor of $\sqrt{2}$, or 1.4. If R or r triples, N increases by a factor of $\sqrt{3}$, or 1.7. It is evident that one should not print three times as many of one book just because it is selling three times as fast as another. Figure 12 shows a plot of R or r against N_{opt}. The slope of this curve, which indicates the sensitivity of N_{opt} to R and r, is

$$\frac{dN_{opt}}{dR} = \sqrt{\frac{K_1}{2R}}; \quad \frac{dN_{opt}}{dr} = \sqrt{\frac{K_2}{2r}}$$

The higher the plant cost of reprinting and the higher the rate of sale, the less sensitive the determination becomes.

But what about p and c? By the same reasoning one sees that N_{opt} is proportional to $1/\sqrt{P}$ and $1/\sqrt{c}$; or

$$N_{opt} = \frac{K_3}{\sqrt{p}}; \quad N_{opt} = \frac{K_4}{\sqrt{c}}$$

If p or c doubles, N_{opt} decreases by a factor of $1/\sqrt{2}$, or 0.7. If p or c triples, N_{opt} decreases by a factor of $1/\sqrt{3}$, or 0.58. It is

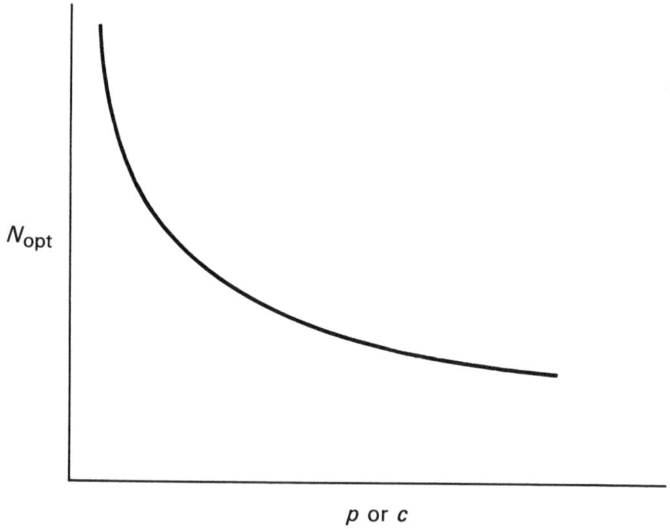

Figure 13

obvious that the higher the unit production cost and the higher the percentage rate of carrying charges, the fewer one will want to print. The shape of the relationship is shown in Figure 13.

The slope of this curve, indicating the sensitivity of N_{opt} to p and c, *is*

$$\frac{dN_{opt}}{dp} = \frac{-K_3}{2\sqrt{p^3}}; \quad \frac{dN_{opt}}{dc} = \frac{-K_4}{2\sqrt{c^3}}$$

The smaller p and c are, the more sensitive their determination becomes. This is not usually a problem with p, since the unit production cost can usually be determined quite accurately before printing begins, but it underlines the importance of a careful periodic study to determine the percentage cost of carrying charges, and it emphasizes the need to keep inventories low when interest rates are high. In the example of a reprinting given earlier ($R =$ \$400, $p =$ \$0.60 per copy, $r = 3000$ copies per year), if c changes from 10% to 8%, the optimum number to print changes from 6300 copies to 7100 copies. The principal components of c are:

1. Interest on investment in inventories (remember that this is investment in production cost only, not plant cost).
2. Percentage cost of warehousing; this is the percentage of the inventory value not including plant cost, not the percentage of the net sales. For this purpose the warehousing cost does not include the run-on costs of picking, packing, and shipping.

APPLICATION: DETERMINING THE QUANTITY TO PRINT

The method described here can serve as a guide to judgment in determining the optimum quantity to order in original printings and reprints. It will not determine *whether* a book will make a profit or loss on a given printing or reprinting. The section on prices and profits, shortly to follow, will discuss this question. It should be pointed out here, however, that if the quantity N_{opt} of a *reprinting* is not sufficient to break even or provide a profit, there is no point in thinking of breaking even or making a profit by printing a larger quantity, since N_{opt} is the optimum. A new book or new edition is another matter, since profits on reprintings may make up for losses on an original printing of an optimum quantity N_{opt}.

For simplicity we have used an example of a book for which the sales tend to decline by 50% per year, starting with a sale of 3000 copies in the first year. This is a fairly typical case for a specialized scholarly book, but other kinds of books would show quite different patterns. Even within a university press list, for example, there are wide variations not only in the quantities sold of different books but in their patterns of sale. It is therefore worthwhile to study the patterns for books with a trade discount and those with a short discount, for books at different prices, for hardbacks and paperbacks, and for books in various fields of knowledge (literary criticism, political science, physics, biology, etc.) to see whether there are significant consistencies and differences that can be taken into account in estimating the market and determining print orders. In fact, now that most publishers have their sales records on computers, it is relatively easy to sort out and develop monthly or yearly averages to produce sales patterns in selected categories. The computer can even be programmed to plot sales curves, if that is desired. The important point is that the formula and the graphical method developed here call the attention of the publisher to the factors on which his decisions should be based, and they require him to study and understand the variables that should be taken into account in making his decisions. Even if he doesn't work out a precise solution in each case, as he probably won't, he should have in mind the nature of that solution and the patterns of sale that are relevant to it.

Finally, and very importantly, it should be kept in mind that a publisher must qualify and modify the decisions indicated by the arguments given here in the light of judgment of other factors not included in this analysis. Is the book becoming obsolete? Does he know of another competing book to be issued soon? What other commitments does he have for his working capital? At what interest rate and how much can he safely borrow if working capital is needed? How certain is he of his sales projections, and how much does he want to hedge?

The calculation of N_{opt} assumes that that number of copies, however it comes out, will actually be sold at the rate predicted. There is no reason to print more than N_{opt}, since by definition the book can be reprinted more cheaply when N_{opt} copies have been sold, *so* N_{opt} *may be regarded as an outside limit to be qualified by other factors,* such as availability of working capital and confidence in future markets. As a matter of policy a publisher may decide never to print more than, say, a three-year supply of any book, regardless of N_{opt}, because he does not want to run risks into the more distant future or because that is the maximum inventory he can afford.

The calculation of N_{opt} for reprints assumes a steady rate of sale. This is often not the case for textbooks and some other books, such as gift books, for which the sale may be very seasonal. In such cases it may be more economical to print just enough (with a small reserve) for the needs of one season and then reprint the next year, rather than carry a whole year's inventory with almost no movement until the next season. And perhaps the market will change before the next season. This does not, of course, invalidate the N_{opt} calculations, but it indicates considerations that would modify the decision on the number to print.

The N_{opt} calculation is most useful as applied to books that are selling quite rapidly and at a fairly steady rate, especially if the unit production cost is high. For example, a popular art book with color plates might have a unit cost of \$2, a plant cost of reprinting of \$2000, and a rate of sale of 5000 copies per year. If the carrying charges are 10%, N_{opt} is 10,000 copies, or a two-year supply.

Even paperback publishers, with low unit costs, may find the N_{opt} calculation helpful. If a quality paperback has a unit cost of \$.50, a rate of sale of 25,000 copies per year, a plant cost of reprinting of \$800, and $c = 10\%$, N_{opt} is 28,200 copies, or a little more than a year's supply. If the rate of sale drops to 15,000 copies per year, N_{opt} is reduced to 21,800 copies, or not quite enough for a year and a half. On the other hand, if the rate is 2000 copies per year, N_{opt} becomes 7900 copies, or nearly four years' supply, and the publisher probably would not want to print that far into the future.

With new books, as we have seen, the situation is even more complex, and the pattern of sale is important. A study of patterns in different subject-matter areas might take the first year's sale as the standard, since this is easier to predict than that of later years, though still full of uncertainties. A graph of patterns of sale would then look something like Figure 14, which is the actual

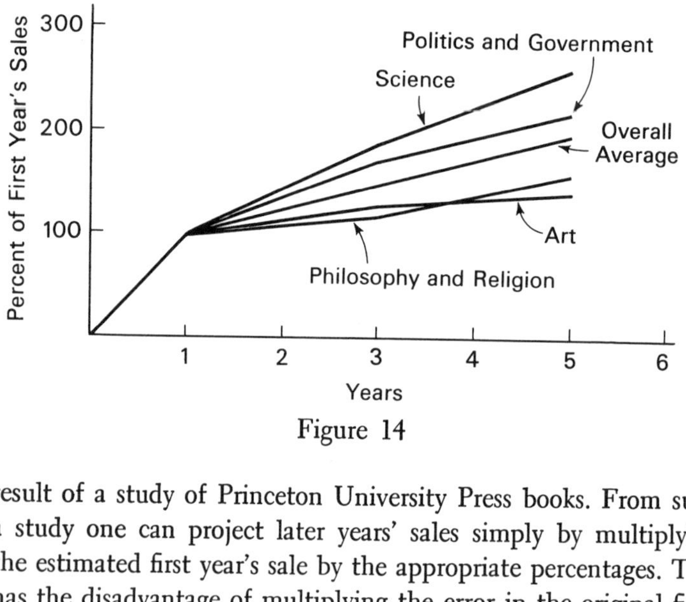

Figure 14

result of a study of Princeton University Press books. From such a study one can project later years' sales simply by multiplying the estimated first year's sale by the appropriate percentages. This has the disadvantage of multiplying the error in the original first-year estimate, so it should be checked against experience with specific similar books. If a policy is established not to print for more than, say, four years, one may prefer to estimate a four-years' sale and project back to the first year, which requires a longer prediction but divides instead of multiplies the error. Either approach provides a pattern from which N_{opt} can be determined, and if a time limit is established it provides a maximum (e.g., a four-year supply) which will be the print order unless N_{opt} is smaller. We shall have more to say about patterns of sale in the section on Prices and Profits below.

KEEPING BOOKS IN STOCK

The application of the formula for N_{opt} is of course not new to publishing. The production manager of one of the larger publishing houses wrote an article on its application in *Publishers' Weekly* a few years ago. A bookseller replied in a letter to the editor saying that if *that* was the way they determined print orders, no wonder the publisher was out of stock so much of the time. The president of the publishing house then wrote a letter of apology and correction to *Publishers' Weekly*, saying that that was *not* the way they set print orders and they were doing their best to keep books in stock. It happens that this publisher publishes an excellent series of books on business management, in which the N_{opt} formula is thoroughly explained; and if the publisher uses some other method, it is because of some of the other conditions discussed here: lack of working capital, uncertainty about future markets, and so forth.

This comedy of errors also emphasizes the idea that the size of the print order is closely related to the number of titles out of stock. Of course, the more often a book has to be reprinted, the more chance there is that the timing of the printing will be wrong and it will be temporarily unavailable. Keeping books in stock is simply a matter of ordering reprintings in time, and this means that the production department must have sufficient warning that a reprint is needed—to get corrections made, to order printing and paper, to arrange for binding, and so forth. There are several standard ways of doing this. Since most publishers now have computerized sales and inventory reports on a monthly or even on a daily basis, they can readily examine the rate of sale in relation to quantity in stock of each title. Some publishers use a system in which a certain minimum level of stock is set for each title; when the stock reaches that level the appropriate manager is notified and a decision on reprinting is made.

A slightly more sophisticated system involves a series of warnings that the stock of a book will soon be exhausted. Rates of sale are estimated from the inventory reports, and the reprint manager is notified perhaps one year, nine months, six months, and three months before the book will be out of stock. This gives the manager time to confer with the editorial department about a possible new edition, to get corrections from the author, to reach a decision on quantity and possible change of price, etc., and finally to issue a reprint order to the production department.

The production manager meanwhile has been getting the periodic notices of dwindling inventory, and when he gets the reprint order he looks to see how much time he has to get the book reprinted. He may have to put it on a rush schedule; or if the stock will not be exhausted for another, say, six months, he holds the reprint order and does not execute it until he gets the three-month notice, which gives him time (but not too much time) to get the reprinting before the book goes out of stock. In a further refinement, the production manager may be under instructions to refer the order back to the reprint manager if more than a certain amount of time (say, four months) passes between receipt of the order and receipt of the three-month notice. Such a delay probably means that there has been a slowing in the rate of sale, and a new decision must be made on whether to reprint and in what quantity.

It is evident from this discussion that a reprint can be ordered too soon, especially if sales are slowing, with the result that money is invested in inventory earlier than necessary and the size of the reprinting will thus probably be larger than necessary. This ultimately leads to write-offs and remaindering.

The opposite situation occurs if reprints are ordered too late; sales are lost because books are unavailable when they are wanted. This can be very serious, especially with a book that is needed for school or college courses; one may lose not only that year's sales but future years', since another book will have been adopted. A wise publisher will take special pains not to let textbooks go out of stock.

But it is wrong to think that every book must be kept continuously in stock until it finally goes out of print; if this is the case, the publisher is certainly ordering reprints too soon. There is a factor of unpredictability in sales rates and to some extent in reprint schedules. A well-managed operation will get most reprints into the warehouse shortly (perhaps a month) before they are needed, but sudden increases in sales rates or delays in reprinting will cause some books to go temporarily out of stock. This number should be held to a reasonable minimum, which will vary among different types of publishers because of different patterns of sale. The publisher must determine what is reasonable from the size of his active list, the typical patterns of sale of his books, his concern for bookstore and author relations, the tightness of his working capital, and so forth. He should also get regular reports on out-of-stock titles, showing how long they have been out of stock and when the reprint is expected. Crucial or badly overdue situations that appear in this report will need investigation and possible action, which also may be required if the report simply lists too many out-of-stock titles.

PRICES AND PROFITS

We have seen that the optimum number to reprint is the quantity for which the accumulated carrying charges (interest on investment, warehousing) will be equal to the plant cost of reprinting (including the cost of making the decision) at the time the edition is exhausted. This quantity is N_{opt}, as discussed earlier in this chapter.

Reprints

In deciding on a reprint, we must next consider *whether* it will pay for itself if the optimum quantity N_{opt} is reprinted. Will the income exceed the costs, and how much will it contribute to overhead?

The manufacturing cost is the plant cost plus the production cost $R + Np$. To this must be added the carrying charges that will be accumulated during the life of the edition, and they must optimally be equal to the plant cost R. Thus the anticipated manufacturing cost plus carrying charges of the reprint edition will be $2R + Np$. These, however, are not all of the costs associated with the reprinting. There are the costs of processing orders in the accounting department and warehouse, the cost of carrying the title in catalogues, and possibly some continuing advertising, and some part of the general overhead which the reprint may be expected to carry.

The unit cost of processing orders in the accounting department and warehouse can be determined by a study of experience. It will vary widely from title to title according to the pattern of ordering; a textbook that sells in groups of fifty or more in August and January is a different matter from a book that sells a few copies every day, mostly single-copy orders. However, a unit cost can be determined for this parameter; we will call it w. Then the total cost for the reprinting will be

$$2R + Np + Nw + O \qquad (4)$$

where O is attributable overhead including advertising, carrying in catalogues, and the like. A publisher may be willing to reprint a book if his costs including overhead are covered, but usually he will want a certain profit, which may be expressed as a percentage of his cost. Thus his minimum criterion for reprinting may be income equal to

$$P\,[2R + N(p + w) + O] \qquad (5)$$

where P is 1.00 + the percent of profit required. If the profit, for example, must be 9% of cost, the expression would be

$$1.09\,[2R + N(p + w) + O] \qquad (6)$$

Obviously, when the receipts from reprinting reach this point, the profit will be 9% beyond cost, or a bit less than 9% of sales. If the publisher is interested in spreading his overhead, $P = 1.00$ may be used.

The income from the sale of the edition will be NSD, where S is the list price and D is the percent of list price returned to the publisher (100% minus discount minus royalty). Thus if the average discount is 30% and the royalty is 10%, $D = 60\%$.

Then, to justify a reprinting, the rate of sale r must be high enough so that

$$N_{opt}SD \geqq P\ [2R + N(p + w) + O] \qquad (7)$$

where N_{opt} is determined by equation (3). It would be possible to substitute equation (3) into equation (7) and solve for the minimum rate of sale that would support a reprinting, but this would be cumbersome. It is more convenient to compute N_{opt} separately and then see whether $N_{opt}SD$ is equal to or greater than $P\ [2R + N(p + w) + O]$. If not, the reprint would not normally be undertaken.

New Books

The case of reprints is usually simple because a reasonably steady rate of sale can be assumed. The rate of sale will probably be affected by the price, and this is where the publisher's judgment and experience must be applied. Various values of S and r may be tried in equations (3) and (7).

The characteristic shape of the relationship between S and r (called a demand curve) for either a new book or a reprint is shown in Figure 15. It is based on the idea that some people (or libraries) will buy a book even at a ridiculously high price; at some ridiculously low price the market begins to be saturated, and sales do not increase very much even though the price is lowered. The product of S and r (shaded area) is the amount of money that the public will spend for the book in a given year at the price *S*. This amount multiplied by *D* (100% less discount and royalty) gives the receipts available to the publisher. The publisher's profit is *SDN* less the costs, including the manufacturing costs, carrying charges, and operating costs.

All these formulas can be applied, as we have seen, equally to a new book or a reprint, but the difficulty with a new book is that one does not know what the rate of sale will be, and the rate will typically change rapidly during the first year or so. Publishers must estimate probable sales and rates of sale as best they can, using their knowledge of the particular new book in relation to past experience with similar books. For this purpose it is useful to have records of the cumulative sale of a variety of books and groups of books, compiled month by month and year by year and plotted cumulatively, as shown in Figures 10 and 14. Rate-of-sale records and plots are also useful, as shown in Figure 16.

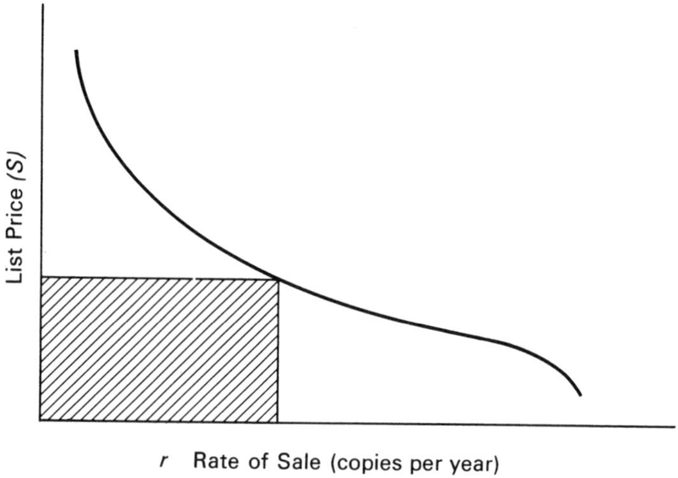

Figure 15

From data of this kind a publisher can infer or estimate a demand curve. A useful approach is to think in terms of the probable sales during the first year of publication, assuming various prices and appropriate sales efforts. Thus for a particular book the curve might be estimated as shown in Figure 17.

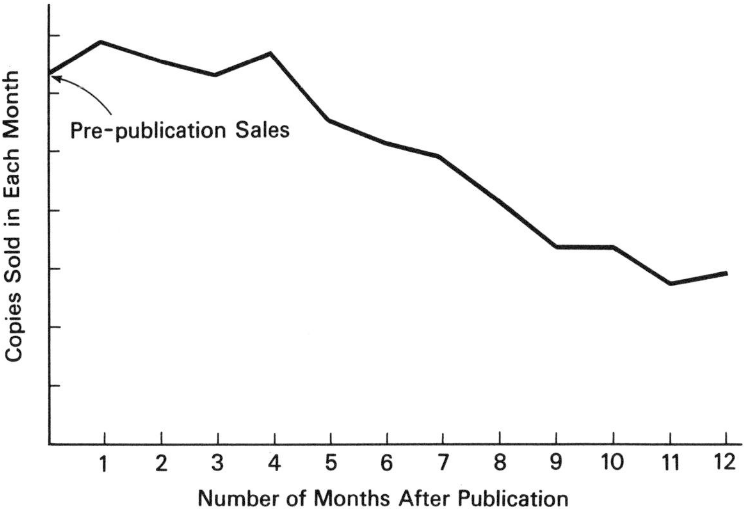

Figure 16

Obviously the demand curve is only a guess, but it should be an informed guess, and the publisher must consider not only experience with other books but the judgments of the editor and the sales manager about the market for the book. Thus the demand curve is a set of probabilities, a kind of vague band, darker in the center indicating higher probability for certain possibilities. This is suggested in Figure 18, where one can see tempting possibilities in the sparse area to the far right and threatening losses in the areas beneath the darkest part of the curve.

Just as the sales pattern will be very different for different types of books (as we saw in Figure 14), the demand curves will be very different, though all will tend to have the basic S shape, dropping steeply, then more gently, and then dropping steeply again. This statement will be modified in situations where different prices and formats enable a book to reach different markets, as discussed later in this chapter (see Figure 31).

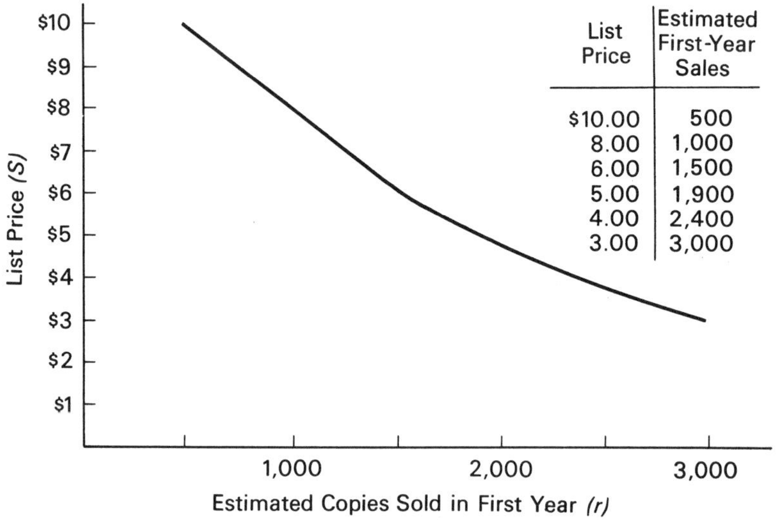

Figure 17

Because it is so difficult to experiment with the price of a book and because each book is different from every other, there is very little firm evidence for any particular demand curve. But some experiments have been tried, primarily by book clubs, and one can see the effects of prices on sales of books in bookstores and in school or other markets. In general, books bought by individuals are much more price-sensitive (the demand curves are flatter) than books bought mainly by institutions like libraries or business firms (the curves are steeper).

It may be objected that the demand curve can be influenced by varying the amount of advertising and selling effort. This is true, but as we have seen in our discussion of advertising and sales budgeting in Chapter III, there is an optimum budget beyond which additional expenditure does not produce a sufficient addition to sales volume. This applies to each individual book, and it can be assumed that the publisher will use his best judgment to determine the optimum advertising and sales effort corresponding to each point on the demand curve. Thus the demand curve plots the estimated sales at various prices, assuming that the optimum advertising and selling effort is made. (Another approach, yielding the same result, would be to plot demand curves assuming various fixed levels of marketing effort; thus a family of curves would be generated, one for each level of marketing effort.)

As we have already seen (Figures 10 and 14), it is helpful to plot patterns of sale for individual books and averages for groups of books, leading to curves like Figure 19. When averages are used, some attention must be paid to the statistical significance of the resulting curve. How many books went into the averages? How wide was the scattering of data? Were there any books

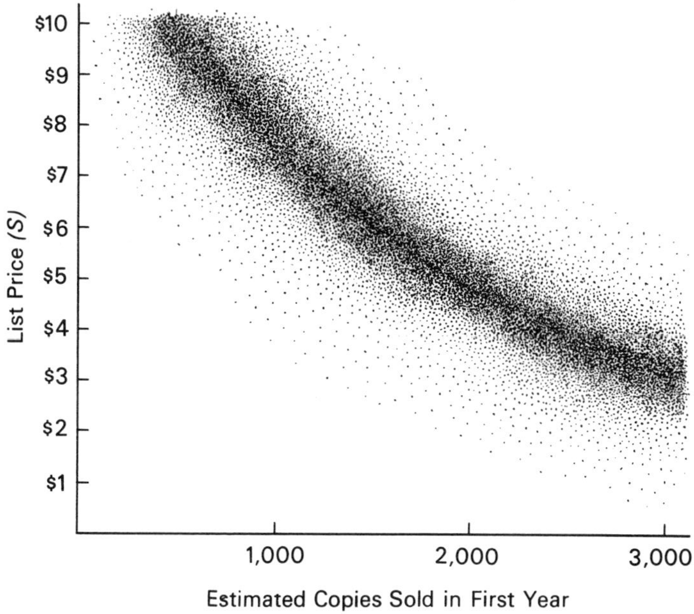

Figure 18

(extremely good or extremely bad sellers) which should be eliminated from the averages to give a more representative pattern? It would of course be possible to apply formal tests of statistical significance, but this would probably not be worthwhile for two reasons: first, even if the statistical significance of such a curve is not great, experience with previous books is *all the experience one has* to apply to future decisions; and second, even if the curve seems quite reliable statistically, the publisher must still apply his judgment to estimate the probable sale of each individual book. Thus sales records of individual books, selected as being similar to a projected book, may be more helpful than averages.

In short, since he must make decisions about quantities and prices, the publisher is forced to estimate a demand curve with

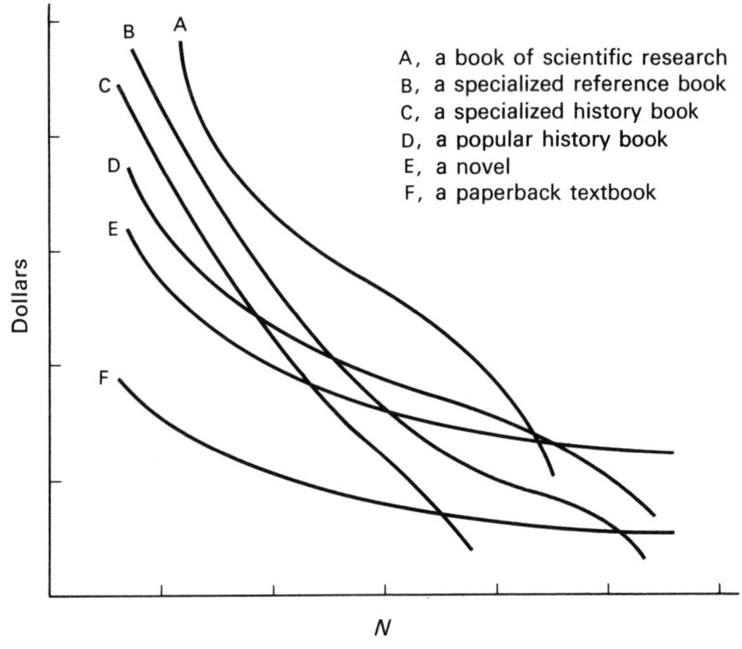

Figure 19

whatever information he can bring to bear. Presumably, the more information he has and uses, the better will be his judgment. He may not actually plot or even consciously imagine a demand curve, but as he considers possible sales prospects and prices, he will in effect be constructing one. The demand curve is the model that represents the demand for a book, against which the pub-

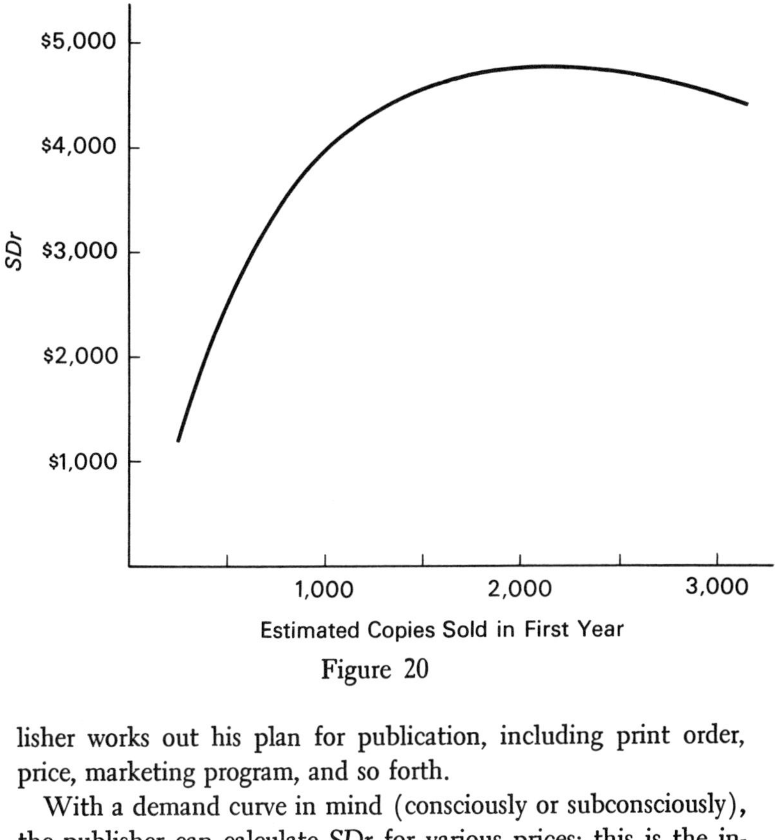

Figure 20

lisher works out his plan for publication, including print order, price, marketing program, and so forth.

With a demand curve in mind (consciously or subconsciously), the publisher can calculate *SDr* for various prices; this is the income against which his costs must be applied. If it is plotted for Figure 17, for example (assuming $D = 50\%$), one gets the curve shown in Figure 20.

The costs can be considered in several parts. First there are the manufacturing costs, consisting of the plant cost plus the number of copies times the unit production cost. This is $R_1 + Np$, as shown in Figure 21. To this must be added the operating cost, which also has a fixed and a variable component. The analysis and allocation of operating costs to individual books will be discussed more fully later in this chapter, but it is enough to point out here

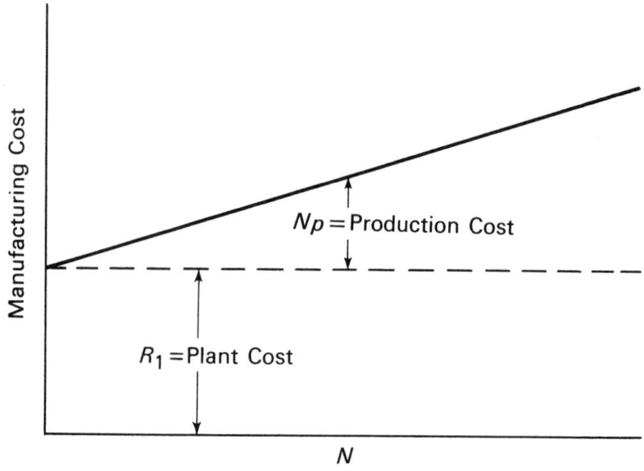

Figure 21

that for any book certain items such as editorial cost and a portion of general overhead will be fixed, while other costs such as shipping, warehousing, order-processing, and sales and advertising will be more nearly proportional to the number of copies printed and sold. Thus the general expression for operating costs will be $E + QN$ where E and Q are the fixed and the unit variable operating costs respectively. The sum is expressed as:

$$\underbrace{R_1 + Np}_{\text{manufacturing}} + \underbrace{E + QN}_{\text{operating}} \quad \text{or} \quad \underbrace{R_1 + E}_{\text{fixed}} + \underbrace{(p + Q)\,N}_{\text{variable}} \tag{8}$$

Finally the carrying charges must be added, and we have seen that these should be equal to the plant cost of reprinting (R_2) over the life of any printing. (Normally the carrying charges would be included in the operating costs; R_2 is added here for completeness. Later in this chapter it is assumed that the carrying charges are part of the operating costs.) The carrying charges will be included with the fixed costs, so for the total costs we get

$$(R_1 + R_2 + E) + (p + Q)\ N \qquad (9)$$

or more simply

$$F + VN \qquad (10)$$

where *F* is the total fixed cost and V is the composite unit variable cost. Then the total cost of publishing a book can be plotted as in Figure 22, where N_{opt} is determined by the method described earlier in this chapter. Then the profit or loss on the first printing can be found by comparing the expression (10) with *SDN* (Figure 20) for N_{opt}. *SDN* is the publisher's revenue from the sale of N copies.

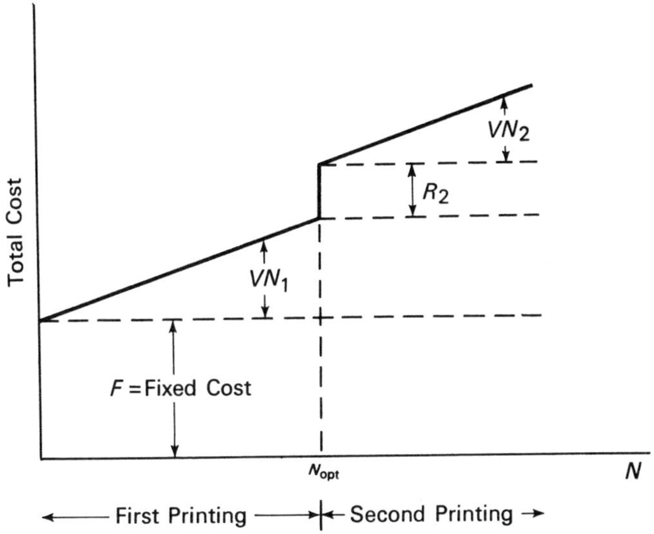

Figure 22

Let us consider further the simple and typical situation in which a publisher expects to make a profit on his first printing, which he hopes to sell in not longer than a certain period, say, two years.

With such a period in mind, the publisher can estimate for book A a demand curve like that in Figure 17. From the demand curve

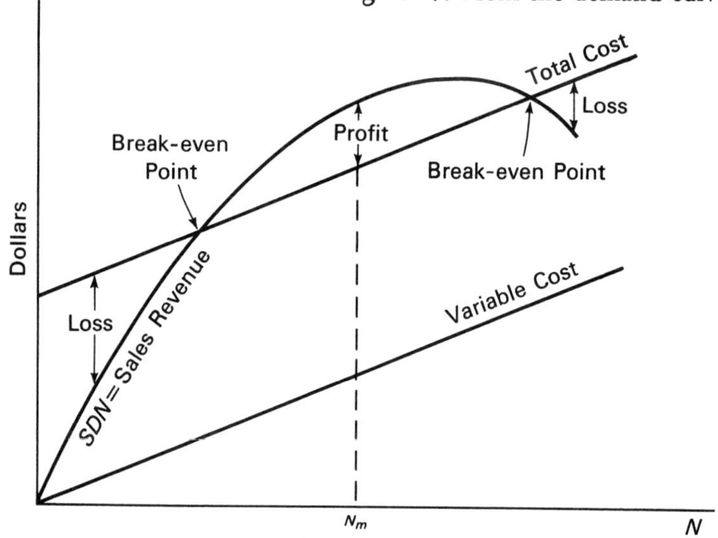

Figure 23

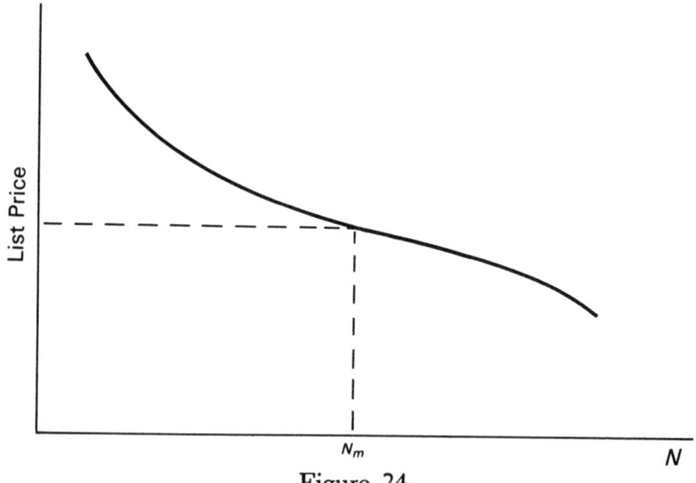

Figure 24

he can project estimates of his sales revenue (*SDN*) at various list prices, as shown in Figure 20. If this projection is compared with costs (Figure 22), the publisher sees something like Figure 23. Seeing that the profit is greatest at N_m, the publisher can look back at his demand curve to find the price that will maximize his profit, assuming that his market estimates are correct (Figure 24).

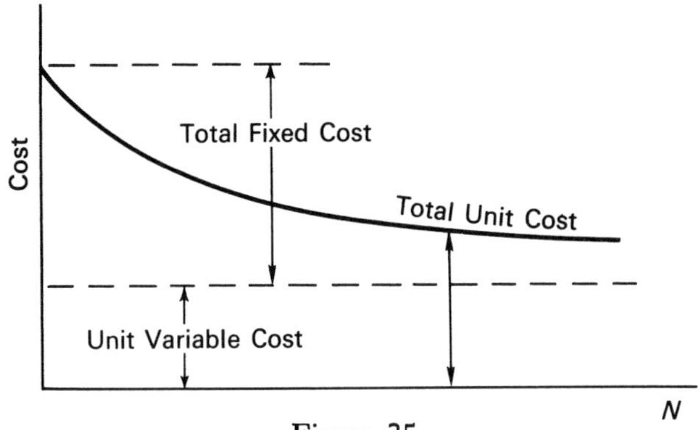

Figure 25

Looking again at Figure 23, one sees that the maximum difference (profit) between the total cost and the publisher's revenue occurs for the same N as the maximum difference between the variable cost and income. In other words, *the optimum price does not depend on fixed costs (including plant cost),* though profit and loss does.*

One might infer from Figure 23 that the maximum-profit point would always occur near the point of maximum sales income.

* Some publishers seem to fix their attention and even base their prices on unit cost *including* fixed cost, but this practice is misleading and can produce bad decisions. It is evident that a large fixed cost is spread more widely over a larger unit cost as the print order increases, so that eventually the unit cost approaches the variable cost, as shown in Figure 25. Publishers issuing small editions, where the "total unit cost" curve is quite steep, can be badly thrown off by this kind of thinking; the variable cost is what matters. This is a reflection of the fact that the customer wants only one copy of the book and does not know or care how many other copies were printed. He compares the price with the prices of other books of similar content and similar size and appearance, that is, of similar variable cost. In other words, he buys in a market and is concerned with price but not with cost; the publisher worries about cost but must recognize that the customer doesn't. An example of the unit-cost approach can be found in "Production Costing with a Formula for Pricing Books," *The Bookseller* (London), Jan. 18, 1969.

This is usually but not always true. For example, consider Figure 26 showing the situation for a book of low plant cost but very high variable cost, such as might occur with a facsimile edition to be produced by color collotype with hand stencilling. In this case the publisher will have a good profit if he puts a very high price on the book and sells N_m copies, but a large loss if he chooses a lower price and sells N' copies, even though his net sales income at N' copies would be greater. This is the usual situation for limited editions produced by hand processes.

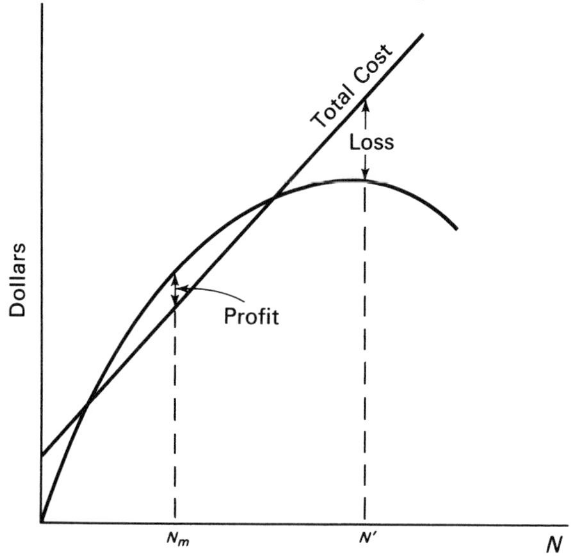

Figure 26

In fact, since costs increase steadily as N increases while the expected revenue first rises and then falls, the publisher's optimum profit point (N_m) always comes at a slightly lower N than maximum revenue. This explains in part why a publisher tends to prefer a higher price while an author will argue for a lower price (corresponding to a larger number of copies sold). Also, authors tend to measure their success in number of copies (readers) than in dollars of royalties.

The advantages of conservative pricing are clearly shown when one plots the profit and loss curve, which is simply the difference between the cost and the revenue; as shown in Figure 23. Thus we have Figure 27. The profit curve is fairly flat to the left of the peak (lower sales and higher price) but falls off steeply into the loss area on the right (higher sales and lower price) because

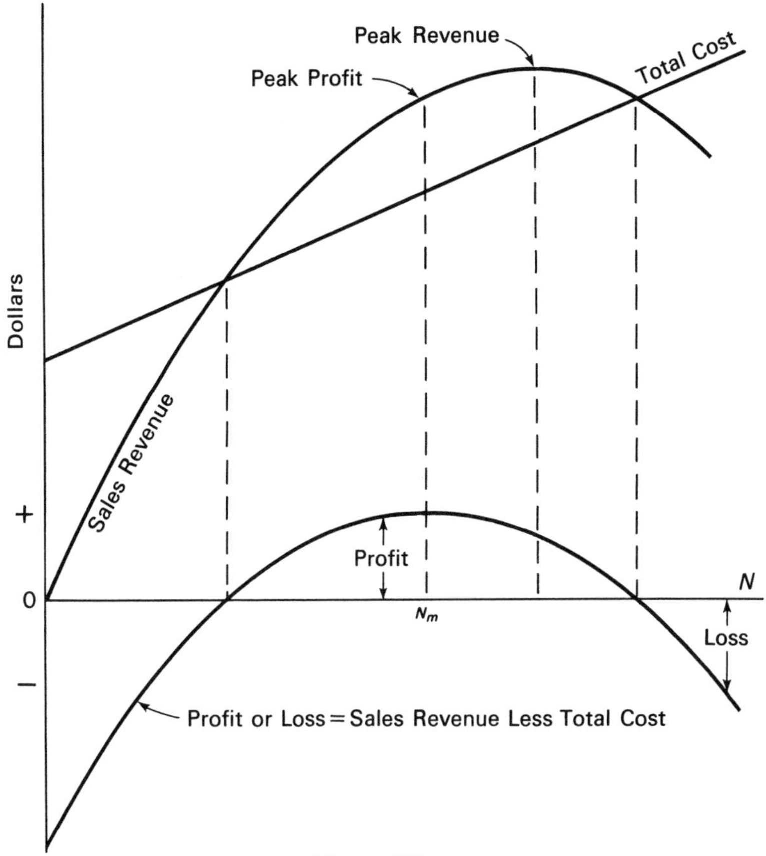

Figure 27

costs are rising and revenues are falling as N increases further. Thus the publisher's uncertainty about the actual determination of the demand curve will cause him to try to stay slightly to the left of N_m. If the demand curve is lower than he has estimated (see Figure 18), he will face serious losses if his price is too low, but probably he will make almost as much profit if his price is slightly on the high side.

Figure 27 also makes it clear that for every book that shows a possibility of profit at all, there will be two breakeven points, one at each of the intersections of cost and revenue, corresponding to different quantities sold at different prices as indicated by the demand curve. Any price between these two breakeven prices will produce some profit. *Once a particular price is chosen,* of course, there is only one breakeven point, unless the plant cost of a reprinting puts the book in the red temporarily, in which case a second breakeven point occurs, as shown in Figure 28.

Sad to say, not every book has even one breakeven point. For some books the cost and revenue diagrams will look not like

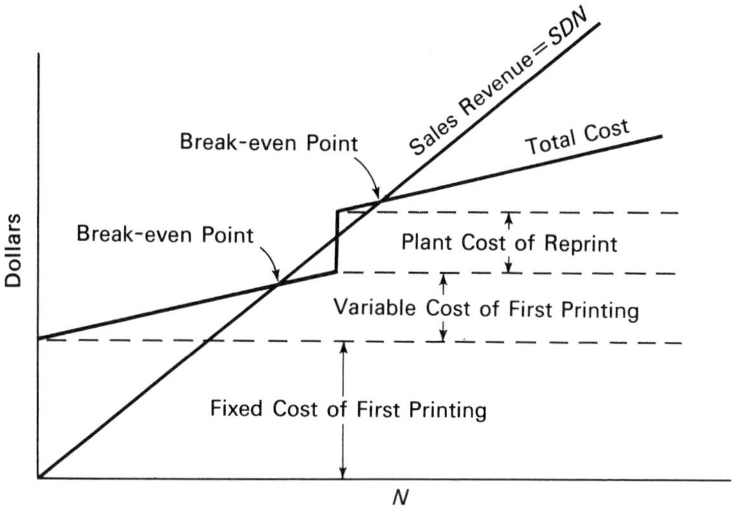

Figure 28

Figure 27 but like Figure 29. For this book *B* there is no price that will enable it to find a sufficient market to pay for the cost. But such books may be intellectually or culturally important and should be published. In such cases, which are common for university presses, the publisher will seek to minimize the loss by choosing the price which enables the revenue to come closest to the cost. Thus he will select the price that corresponds to N_m, as shown, and will probably try to find a subsidy to cover the esti-

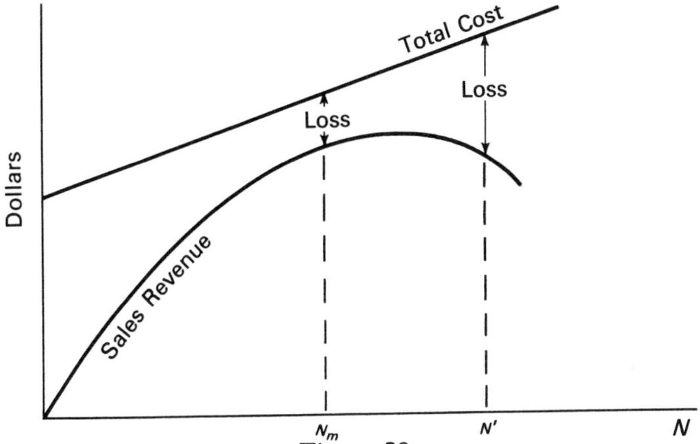

Figure 29

mated loss. Sometimes a sponsor will want to subsidize a lower price in order to make it possible to sell more copies; that is, he will want to push the number out, say, to N' on the diagram. Since cost is rising and revenue is falling in this area of the diagram, the sponsor (or the publisher, if he is unwary) may be surprised to find how much it costs to subsidize a lower price.

Before leaving this discussion of micro-publishing profit and loss, it is important to note that it is quite possible to lose money on the first printing and still make money on reprintings. To see this graphically, consider Figure 30, which shows the receipts available to the publisher (*SDN*) in relation to the total cost of a book with a high fixed publication cost, a low plant cost of reprinting, and a high rate of sale. In this case N_{opt} is low and occurs before the book can break even; it is nevertheless the optimum number for a first printing. But as the book is reprinted a number of times, it moves into the profit area. One can determine the most profitable list price by locating the place where the distance between total cost and receipts is maximum, reading down to N_m, and going back to the demand curve to read off the list price that corresponds to N_m.

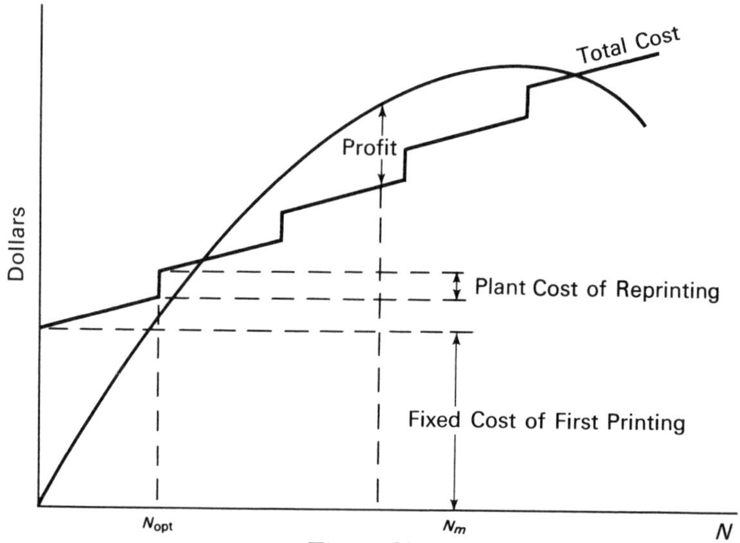

Figure 30

We keep coming back to the demand curve, the publisher's estimate of how many copies can be sold in a given time at a given price—in short, his estimate of the market. But it should be remembered that the book market is not homogeneous; it is a cluster of different markets for different books at different prices, to be reached in different ways. Thus one speaks of the library market, the school market, the college market, the paperback market, and so forth. The existence of different markets sometimes leads to sharp bends amounting almost to discontinuities in the demand curve. For example, a long biography of a world figure might sell quite well at $12.50, and that might seem to be the optimum price, but $12.50 might be thought to keep the book out of the gift market at Christmas; people often think of ten dollars (a ten-dollar bill) as a limit on what they will spend for a book. If they are spending more, they want an art book with colored illustrations. So perhaps lowering the price to \$10 would increase the sales enormously, while \$10.50 (an odd price!) would not. This produces a virtual discontinuity, as shown in Figure 31. Then if the price is lowered still more, the projected sales increase only gradually until, for example, one gets to \$7.50, where the book begins to be used in college history courses and another big jump in sales occurs. In this market, decreasing the price will again produce gradual increases in sales, but if one goes down, say, to \$2.95 and issues the book in paper covers, one can reach what is called the quality-paperback market and another big jump occurs. Finally, if one goes all the way to 95 cents in paper covers on newsprint, with appropriate marketing efforts, the so-called mass market can be reached. These books are sold in drugstores, railway stations, and airports (not usually in book-

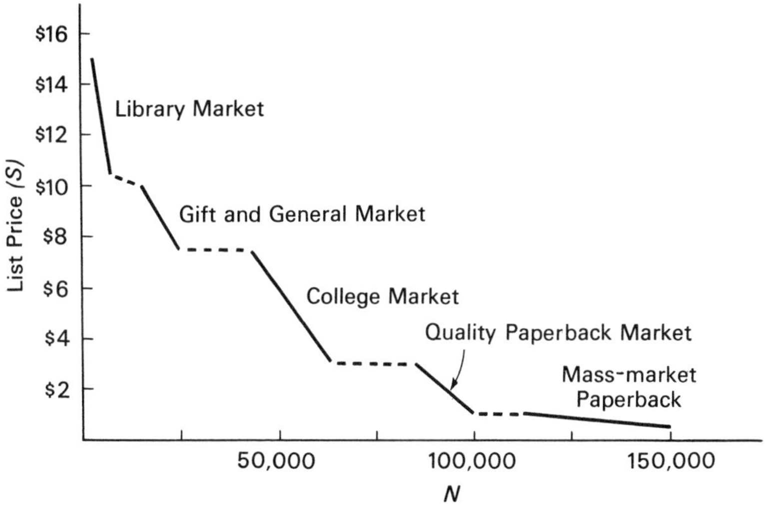

Figure 31

stores) and are marketed by specialized publishers with magazine-type distribution networks to many people who rarely read hardback books. In recent years there have been an increasing number of bookstores carrying paperbacks exclusively. Those near college campuses carry mainly the higher priced "quality" paperbacks; those in heavily traveled locations (airports, railroad stations) carry mainly the mass-market paperbacks.

In short, such a book has several different markets, and a wise publisher will try to reach all of them eventually, timing his efforts so as to maximize his return. He might decide, for example, to publish the book in early September at $10 at a trade discount in order to reach the general and gift market before Christmas. He would plan an energetic advertising campaign in general media, perhaps with appropriate publicity involving the author (radio and television appearances, and so forth). In the following spring he might issue a textbook edition with a different binding at a $7.50 price and a 20% discount, with a direct mail campaign to college teachers, offering "examination copies," hoping for wide course adoptions in the following fall. He might continue with these two editions, trade and text, for a year or so, depending on the continuation of college adoptions. Eventually he would probably put out his own quality-paperback edition, knowing that this would completely supersede his text edition but expecting to reach a much wider college and general market. When that edition is established, he might lease the reprint rights to a mass-market paperback publisher, thus reaching the drugstore and airport market and probably not interfering greatly with the established college market which channels through bookstores.

Thus, by sequentially exploiting the various markets, as indicated by the discontinuities of the demand curve, the publisher maximizes his and the author's return from publication of the book. Or it may not be necessary to publish for different markets sequentially. Often parallel editions, issued simultaneously, can exist side by side without interference: a hardbound trade edition, a quality paperback for college courses, a mass-market paperback for the drugstore market. And, of course, most books do not have the potential to reach all these different markets, and are published in one form only. In estimating markets, there is plenty of room for judgment based on experience.

Figure 31 makes the point, which is sometimes seemingly forgotten, that the paperback market ("quality" or "mass") is a part of the total market for a book, not something entirely separate. A paperback book is simply a book with paper covers, and often clothbound and paperbound editions are identical except for the bindings. Thus the unit cost will vary only by the cost of the binding, perhaps 50¢, while the prices may be, for example, $1.95 and $7.50—or the difference may be even greater. This apparently artificial price variation, not reflecting differences in cost, is an example of the economics of product differentiation in order to reach different markets; that is, different expectations and demands from the public. The hardbound edition is almost always issued first, and for most titles will be the only edition. Cloth bindings are wanted for books that will have hard use, such as textbooks or reference books, and for large, heavy books and for books for library use or for gifts. Most review media give major attention only to hardbacks. Moreover, as we have seen, the difficulty of estimating the market for a new book and a cost structure that includes large fixed costs tend to make the publisher print and price conservatively, which means a small hardbound edition at a relatively high price. The success of the hardbound book will pay the fixed costs and at the same time tend to create the larger demand that will justify a paperback edition.

Theoretically it might be said that the publisher could simply lower the price of the hardback to, say, $2, and reach the paperback market, but this is not the case. The format is symbolic of the market, which also means the channels of distribution. There are wholesalers and bookstores that specialize in paperbacks, there are professors who will assign only paperbacks to their students, and there are people who go to bookstores looking only for paperbacks. A cheap clothbound book is not the same, and will not go through the same channels. Thus the format of the book is part of the marketing picture, and an appropriate format is essential.

I have illustrated the importance of format with reference to hardbacks and paperbacks, but format is important in many other ways. In estimating the demand curve the publisher must have a mental picture of the book in mind, or he must choose a format or formats that will be right for the market or markets that he seeks. A gift book must look worthy as a gift, flattering both the giver and the receiver, and a well-designed jacket can be enormously effective in catching attention and encouraging interest. Some books must be large to accommodate pictures or make a certain impression, while others should be small and neat. The publisher has great latitude in choosing a format for any particular book: he can compress it to make it less formidable and to save money on printing and paper and binding, or he can expand the number of pages to justify a higher price. Obviously, the choice of a format has effects on manufacturing costs which must be taken into account as the plan for publication is developed.

We have already seen that in estimating the demand curve, the publisher must keep in mind that marketing effort is a variable, and he must include an appropriate marketing effort for each level of sales in his computation of costs. For certain types of books, especially professional and scholarly books, there is a definite market that can be saturated with a well-aimed marketing effort; for such books the demand curve is relatively easy to visualize. For many other books, especially books appealing to the general public, the sales may be more sensitive to the marketing effort, and in comparing revenue with costs the publisher will have to allow for larger marketing expenditures if he is to reach a larger market.

In short, the demand curve assumes an appropriate level of marketing effort for each level of distribution achieved. This is, of course, a matter for publishing knowledge and judgment and experience—but this whole discussion is meant only to supplement knowledge and judgment and experience, certainly not to replace it. And in any case the entire determination of a demand curve is based on knowledge and judgment and experience. Even with the best judgment there will be uncertainties and imponderables—such as the reception of the book by reviewers, or the space allotted (in competition with other books) in the review media, or the possibility of special publicity, and so forth. To some extent, the careful analysis we have been doing is something like a horse player's analysis of a racing form. One still has to know the horses and the jockeys and sometimes play hunches.

SUMMARY ON PRINT ORDERS AND PRICES

The foregoing somewhat technical consideration of micro-publishing can be summarized as follows:

1. The optimum quantity to print of a new book or a reprint is such that the carrying charges, by the time the printing is sold out, will equal the plant cost of reprinting. The formula that expresses this is

$$N_{opt} = \sqrt{\frac{2Rr}{pc}}$$

Thus, other things being equal, the print order will vary as the square root of the plant cost of reprinting and of the rate of sale, and as the reciprocal of the square root of the unit production cost and of the rate of carrying charges.

If two books have the same unit production cost and the same rate of sale and if the plant cost of reprinting of one is twice that of the other, one should print 1.4 (or $\sqrt{2}$) times as many of the one that has the higher plant cost of reprinting.

Likewise, if other things are equal and one book is selling twice as fast as another, one should print 1.4 (or $\sqrt{2}$) times as many of the faster selling book (*not* twice as many!).

If the plant cost of reprinting and rates of sale of two books are equal and one has twice the unit production cost of the other, one should print 0.7 (or $1/\sqrt{2}$) times as many of the more costly one as of the less costly one. [This is the same thing as saying that one should print 1.4 (or $\sqrt{2}$) times as many of the *less* costly one.]

2. The optimum price for a book is that which will maximize the profit or minimize the loss when the total publishing cost is compared with the estimated publisher's revenue computed from a demand curve.

3. Both the optimum price and the optimum print order are affected by the variable cost, while neither is at all affected by fixed costs such as plant costs.

4. In spite of Item 3, the profit or loss on a book depends heavily on various categories of fixed costs.

5. A plan for publication of a book must include appropriate and sufficient marketing effort to reach the particular market or markets intended, and the budget must include an allowance for such an effort.

6. There is plenty of room for judgment in weighing the relevant factors, but technical analysis should serve as a guide to judgment. A wise publisher will hedge his bets. He will not plan his edition too far into the future, especially if he has a problem of sufficient working capital. He will tend to price a book slightly higher than the optimum price indicated by an estimate of demand, realizing the uncertainty of such estimates and aware of steepness of the loss curve if demand is overestimated and books are underpriced.

OPERATING COSTS APPLICABLE TO AN INDIVIDUAL BOOK

The approach taken here requires the publisher to think in terms of the total cost of publishing an individual book. Some publishers would say that this is not necessary, and indeed in theory one should be able to decide what to publish by choosing the books that contribute the most revenue beyond the increase in cost (manufacturing and operating) caused by publishing that book. That is, one compares the marginal revenue to the marginal cost. But unless a house has most of its work done on a freelance basis, by the job (as a small house, just beginning, might do), one does not usually confront the problem in this way. In a going concern the publisher has certain operating expenses, especially salaries, that are bound to be incurred; and in order to think consistently about publishing projects, he must have some reasonable way of assigning operating costs to them, in order to get an approximate figure for the total cost of publication and to be sure that at the end of the year there will be enough revenue to cover costs and provide a profit.

In our earlier discussions of the economics of micro-publishing, we saw that the operating cost and the manufacturing cost each consisted of fixed costs and variable costs. The fixed manufacturing cost is called plant cost and the variable manufacturing cost is called production cost, so the total manufacturing cost is $R_1 + Np$, as shown in Figure 21. We also saw that the operating costs can be divided into fixed and variable, which appeared in the form $E + QN$ in expression (8), and we said that the details of the analysis and allocation of operating costs to individual titles would be discussed later. That is our task now, and we must begin by classifying the operating-expense items on the typical operating statement discussed in Chapter III. Let us group them as shown in Table II.

TABLE II. OPERATING COSTS

A. Related to the length of a book (number of pages)
   1. Editorial expense
   2. Design department (especially if illustrated)

B. Related to the number of copies printed or sold
   1. Production department (more reprintings)
   2. Selling expense
   3. Advertising and promotion expense, excluding out-of-pocket advertising costs
   4. Shipping and warehousing expense

C. Fixed costs not directly related to *A* or *B* (general and administrative)

D. Out-of-pocket advertising costs

This is a rather crude classification, and an experienced publisher will immediately see that a large part of editorial expense, in fact nearly all except for copyediting, is not related to the number of pages in a book and that work in the design and production departments is only very roughly related to the length and number of copies respectively. Nevertheless, if these expenses are to be allocated to individual books for the purpose of estimating total costs, this division is useful. Thus the expression for the operating cost of publishing an individual book might be

$$Ag + BN + C + J \tag{11}$$

where A = a cost related to the length of a book
B = a cost related to the number of copies printed
C = an allocation of fixed costs
J = the advertising budget for the book
g = the number of pages in the book
N = the number of copies to be printed

It should be noted that since Table II includes all the operating-cost items from the operating statement, carrying charges are included in item C, so it is not necessary to add R_2 as carrying charges, as shown in expression (9).

Method I. In the simplest case A might be obtained by dividing the total of the budget items under A in Table II by the number of pages expected to be published during the year (or expected to be processed by the editorial and design departments). B might be obtained by dividing the items under B in Table II by the number of *copies* of new books and reprints expected to be printed (or sold) during the year. C might be determined by dividing the total general and administrative costs by the number of new books and reprints (titles) expected to be issued during the year. And J could be the actual out-of-pocket advertising of the book budget allocated on the basis of experience and knowledge of the book.

The strict application of expression (11), with parameters developed as described above, would be a logical way to allocate operating costs. But I doubt whether any publisher does it this way, and this method is probably not even desirable without modification. A principal difficulty arises in the allocation of the fixed costs C. C is a special problem because it is the book's share of the general overhead and administrative costs, and there is no truly logical way of allocating it; anything one does with C is arbitrary. Should each book carry the same amount of overhead (as in Method I)? Should big books with high prices carry more overhead than small books with low prices? Should books that sell in large quantities carry more overhead than books that sell in small quantities? The overhead and administrative expenses are large, usually amounting to 15% to 20% of the total costs; how one allocates them may make a significant difference in the other decisions one makes. Methods II and III provide ways of allocating more fixed overhead to large books (carrying high prices) and to those printed in large quantities, and less to small books and to books printed in small quantities.

Method II. Another approach might be not to allocate these costs to individual books at all; using as an operating-cost formula only

$$Ag + BN + J, \tag{12}$$

the difference between the expected income and the total cost becomes not profit, but "amount contributed to overhead and profit." The publisher can set a minimum standard percentage for this in terms of net receipts. Thus he might say, "I will not publish a book unless I can expect that it will contribute at least 25% of its net receipts, beyond manufacturing cost and operating cost [calculated by expression (12)] to general overhead and profit." If he does this he will be setting up the situation shown in Figure 32. The price will not be affected, since 75% *SDN* has the same basic shape as *SDN*. If the cost line touches the 75% *SDN* line at all, the publisher can expect that the book will produce the minimum designated profit.

The difficulty with this method is that the amount of general overhead allocated to any individual book is proportional to the net receipts for that book. Thus the overhead allocation to a book is affected by its price and estimated sales, a situation that does not accord with reality. In planning publication of a book, one would like to be able to say that the total operating cost is a certain definite amount (like the manufacturing cost), regardless of what price one chooses or how many are actually sold. Nevertheless, Method II is a reasonable procedure.

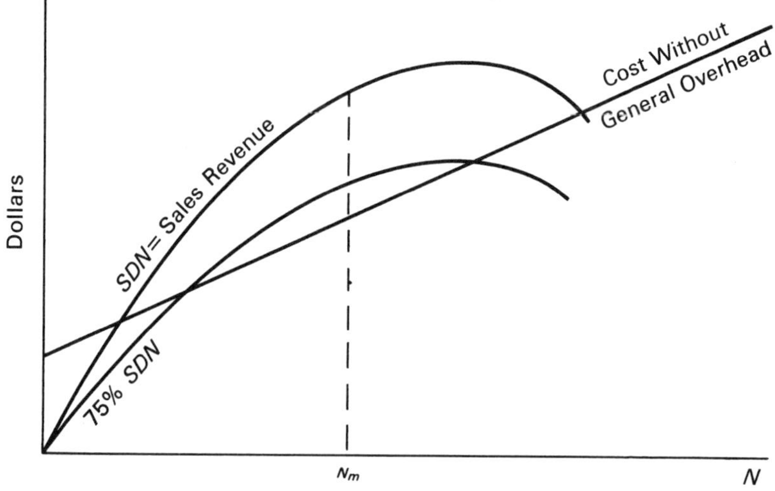

Figure 32

Method III. A third method, which has the advantage of giving a definite operating cost for each book, is to allocate a part of the general overhead to the *A* and *B* factors when calculating the parameters, leaving a certain fixed minimum for each title. Thus one-third of the general overhead cost might be added to the *A* items before dividing by the number of pages, and another third might be added to the *B* items before dividing by the number of copies printed (not sold), leaving a third of the general overhead cost to be assigned equally to each title. This would produce a result like that shown in expression (11), but it would allocate more overhead to big books with high prices and to books expected to sell in large quantities.

Most houses, especially large ones, prefer to allocate overhead costs in proportion to net receipts, and in fact many publishers simply estimate all operating costs on this basis even though it produces large distortions in planning the publication of individual books. Smaller publishing houses have a greater need for precise planning of individual projects, so Methods II or III, perhaps with variations to suit particular needs, would be better for them. University presses in particular, since they must often justify needs for subsidies or explain financial problems to authorities unfamiliar with publishing, should find Method III attractive, since it is easy to explain and produces a definite figure, independent of price or expected sales, for the estimated operating cost. Thus with Method III, the allocated operating cost for a new book is

$$Ag + BN + C + J$$

where A is dollars per page, B is dollars per copy, C is a fixed allocation of general overhead, and J is the out-of-pocket advertising budget for the book.

For a reprint the allocated operating cost would be

$$BN + C + J$$

since there are no costs in the A category associated with reprints, and J would often be very small or zero.

In sum, it is desirable to allocate as much of the operating costs to a particular book as can be specifically identified with that book, but there will always be a large portion of operating costs that are not allocable except on some fairly arbitrary basis. How these general operating expenses are allocated will depend on the particular situation. In a sense, assuming that a publisher is going to publish a certain round number of books each year, it doesn't matter what method is used; the publisher can simply choose those books that will contribute most to overhead and profit, beyond the specifically identifiable manufacturing and other costs (sometimes called the "get-out costs"). But many publishers, especially smaller publishers and publishers of small editions, need more specific figures for specific projects; in such cases the methods discussed here should be helpful.*

FROM MICRO-PUBLISHING TO MACRO-PUBLISHING

The discussion of the allocation of operating costs to individual titles in order to work out micro-publishing profit and loss and to determine print orders and prices has taken us back again to macro-publishing in the form of the operating statement. We see that the cost of the flow of macro-publishing activity must be broken down, in part arbitrarily, to make micro-publishing decisions. But the very fact that the breakdown is somewhat arbitrary, to be worked out by each publisher in accordance with his particular problems and objectives, itself indicates the cohesiveness of the publishing program as a whole. In many respects each new book is a new venture and must be considered as such, but it is also a part of a larger flow, and the way it is treated will depend substantially on the characteristics of the publishing house.

DISCOUNTS

Earlier in this chapter the subject of discounts was passed over rather quickly. In expression (7), *D* was introduced as "the percent of list price returned to the publisher (100% minus discount

* After reading this section, and with reference to the operating ratio reports discussed in Chapter III, Daniel Melcher commented, "If I were to be confronted with so large a figure for G&A I would ask to have it further broken down. I like to get this kind of outlay reduced to *truly* unallocable amounts, and then *not to allocate it at all,* ever. This makes for unhappy accountants, but it also breaks up their little game of telling you that a project is showing a loss, when in fact, you would be far worse off without it." This comment is entirely consistent with and in the spirit of this section.

minus royalty)," and *NSD* (where *N* is the number sold and *S* is the list price) is the publisher's revenue available to pay manufacturing and operating costs. We shall now consider discount as a separate subject before going on to consider royalties.

A quick look at *Publishers' Trade List Annual* or *American Booksellers Association Handbook* will reveal that discount is a complicated topic. Publishers' discounts vary in a thousand ways. In fact, fair-trade legislation forbids publishers (and others) to agree on discounts, so each publisher makes his own discount schedule. However, since publishers are selling generally through bookstores and wholesalers to the same markets, there is a large degree of consistency and similarity in spite of the variations.

If a publisher wants his books displayed in bookstores, he must offer the bookseller enough discount to make it worthwhile to order and stock the book. In general the bookstores need at least a 40% discount, though they can manage with 33⅓% on high-priced technical books. The publisher wants the bookstore to carry a large stock of his books, so he offers inducements in the form of higher discounts for larger orders, perhaps ranging up to 46% or in some cases even to 50% for large-quantity assortments. And he discourages single-copy orders by giving only 33⅓% or less on them. This is the general pattern, with the average discount ranging from 40% to 45%. Wholesalers may get slightly higher discounts, though many publishers have a single discount schedule for both bookstores and wholesalers, and wholesalers get larger discounts only by ordering in quantity. Publishers will usually give libraries a special discount of 10% or more, so a wholesaler who sells mainly to libraries can order multiple copies at perhaps 45% discount and resell to libraries at substantial discounts and still make a profit.

Some kinds of books are sold mainly through other means than bookstores. Elementary and high school textbooks, for example, are sold directly to school systems at net prices; in the few states where there are still statewide textbook adoptions, publishers bid against each other to supply textbook series in standard subjects. College textbooks are sold mainly through bookstores, usually college bookstores, but the bookstore does not have to make any substantial effort or investment to get the sale; it simply orders stock of the books required by the professors, fills the students' requests, and returns the unsold copies. For this reason lower discounts prevail for college textbooks, usually 20%.

Paperbacks are a different matter, though many are used as required or recommended reading in college courses and an increasing number are being published at standard text (short) discounts. But most paperbacks are sold from display stands, and full trade discounts are required, 40% or more, depending on the quantity ordered.

An investigation of publishers' discount schedules will reveal many further categories and variations, but the point here is that the publisher is in the marketplace to sell his books, and he must offer enough discount to make his books attractive wherever he wants to sell them. He is in competition for the limited working capital of the bookseller and wholesaler, for the book-buying budgets of libraries, and for the textbook budgets of school systems and of individual students. He will not offer more discount than he must, but he must meet the competition in the book trade. Within a publisher's list there will be several categories of discounts (trade, text, paperback, etc.) and the same book may be sold at several discounts depending on the quantity ordered and the customer (bookstore, wholesaler, library, etc.). From time to time a publisher will adjust his discount schedule, and in any case the proportion of his sales in various categories or sold to various kinds of customers will change. Accordingly the publisher will need to make periodic studies of average discounts for different categories of books in order to establish the factor D to be used in calculating his projected revenue. But to establish D he will also have to look at royalties.

ROYALTIES

So little has been said about royalties in the earlier discussion that one might think they were not important—but of course they are. Royalties are what the author is paid for the intelligence, imagination, and hard work that have gone into writing his manuscript; without the author there would be no book, and of course the author deserves to be paid.

Royalties are the standard method of paying the author—a percentage of the list price (or sometimes of the publisher's net receipts from sales) on all copies sold. Thus the author is usually paid in proportion to sales and in proportion to the price of his book. Although there is a slight tendency for the publisher to price a book higher than its author might wish, as already pointed out, their interests are essentially the same. Once the price is set, the publisher wants to sell as many books as possible, and the author's royalties will be in proportion to his success.

What percentage royalty should the author receive? The answer, for an author, is as much as possible. Royalty rates do not vary greatly from publisher to publisher, and most publishers have a standard rate at something like 10% of the list price on the first 5000 copies sold, 12½% on the next 5000 copies, and 15% beyond 10,000 copies. But such standard rates are often broken for particular authors, in the face of competition from other publishers. Publishers *do* compete for authors, and royalty rates are one area of competition. Another area is advances on royalties, and sometimes, when a publisher wants to compete strongly, he will offer an advance payment that is more than the book is likely to earn at the standard rate; since the advance is in the nature of a guarantee, this enables him to compete without technically exceeding his standard rate. Publishers do not like to break their standard rates—the word gets around—but it is primarily a question of the marketplace. So the author will try to get the best royalty provisions he can, other things being equal—but other things are rarely equal. An author will often have a preference or an established relationship with a publisher; he will have confidence that a particular publisher will edit his book more sensitively, will produce a handsomer finished product, or will advertise and sell more effectively, and these will also be important considerations.

Since these are considerations for an author, they are also considerations for a publisher. We have already looked at some of these matters in Chapter III in the discussion of the decision to proceed with publication. The publisher is in the marketplace as a buyer of manuscripts, and he will compete with royalties, advances, and services in accordance with his judgment.

At this point something should be said about the simultaneous submission of a manuscript to several publishers, an approach sometimes used by authors and agents but one frowned on by publishers, since it puts them in direct competition and since the consideration of a manuscript is expensive and time-consuming. But there is really nothing to object to, *provided* that the publisher is told that the manuscript is also being considered elsewhere. This is only fair. It tells the publisher that he is in direct competition for the manuscript, and it leaves him a choice of actions: to reject immediately or after a preliminary scanning, or to compete energetically with offers of large advances and high royalty rates. Thus simultaneous submission may be advantageous to an author with a highly salable manuscript, but it is surely disadvantageous to an author who wants his manuscript considered carefully and whose manuscript is probably acceptable only to a publisher who fully appreciates its real substance. Most publishers will not put in the necessary effort to reach a decision on such manuscripts if they think they may be outbid by another publisher eventually anyway.

So we return to the marketplace to set royalty rates, whether a manuscript is submitted simultaneously or not. And the marketplace operates in either case because a publisher cannot afford to get a reputation for being tight with authors. A publisher does not just compete for a single manuscript; he is establishing a relationship with an author who he hopes will bring him future manuscripts, and whenever he deals with an author he is building (or tearing down) his reputation. Each publisher develops his own policies and style in dealing with authors, and royalty rates are an important but by no means decisive aspect. It was for this reason that Saxe Commins, the great editor at Random House, used to say that a bad contract with a good publisher was better than a good contract with a bad publisher. Best of all, of course, is a good contract with a good publisher—and, in fact, a good publisher is likely to make a good contract.

THE PUBLICATION PLAN

In Chapter III we discussed the probable composition of a committee to decide on the acceptance or rejection of manuscripts, and we said that each would be considered in terms of a carefully worked-out publication plan. The discussion of the economics of micro-publishing in this chapter provides the basis for such a plan.

When the publisher or one of his colleagues sits down to draw up a publication plan, he probably brings to the task a great deal of information and experience that is mostly subconscious; it is the result of years of immersion in publishing and an accumulation of background knowledge of individual books and of the history of the publishing house that have become second nature to him. He does not have to analyze the relationships and variables that we have been discussing, any more than a fish has to analyze the water of the stream in which he swims. In fact, if he has grown up in publishing, he may never have thought through such an analysis in detail; he may simply have learned trade practices by observation and absorbed enough to be able to sense publishing possibilities and to make good decisions almost by instinct. Instinct and experience are invaluable; however, evolution has recorded the extinction of many species with highly developed instincts but with little ability to adapt quickly enough to changing situations. Publishing is changing rapidly today, and the publisher who adds to his instinct and experience an element of fresh analysis is more likely to be able to make decisions that will produce the desired results.

Thus the publisher will have in mind, as he works on the

publication plan for a particular book, the interplay of price, cost, print order, discount, royalty, and estimated demand. And he will also have in mind the particular situation and problems of his publishing house as a whole: Is the inventory too high? Is the working capital sufficient? Is there an effort to develop certain kinds of publications? What are the royalty and discount policies? . . . and so forth. All these matters may not come explicitly or consciously into play as he works out his plan, but they will be in mind and will affect the plan.

So—here is this publishing project. Here are the reports of editors and advisers. Here is the manuscript which the publisher has at least sampled or preferably read completely. Here is a cost estimate from the production department; information about the author, including data on his previous books; comments and estimates of sales from the marketing department; sales records of other books in the same field. And so forth. Should the book be accepted for publication? If so, how should it be published?

Having read the reports of editors and advisers, the publisher looks at the manufacturing estimate, which shows that the book will make 352 pages in a 5½- by 8½-inch format, set 10 on 12 in Baskerville, printed on 50-pound antique-finish paper, bound in B-grade cloth, with a jacket printed in three colors, etc. From the specifications on the manufacturing estimate, the publisher forms in his mind a picture of the proposed book as a physical object, imagining how it will look in the bookstore to the particular readers for whom it is intended. He wonders briefly whether the book should be illustrated and notes that the editor has not recommended any illustrations.

Looking at the memo from the sales manager and glancing over the sales records of earlier books by the same author in comparison to the sales of other similar books, he wonders how many copies of the book would be sold in the first year of publication if the price were, say, $6. And what if the price were $7.50, or perhaps $6.95? He reviews the sales manager's estimate of sales and comments on price. He has already subconsciously decided, from the nature of the content and the kind of expected readership, that the book should carry a trade discount so that it can be displayed in bookstores, and he knows that on earlier books the author has received the house's standard scaled royalty rate, beginning at 10% and increasing to 12½% and 15% at 5000 and 10,000 copies, so he does a little preliminary arithmetic, as follows:

Quantity	*Average discount*	*Royalty*	*Price*	*Sales revenue*
5000	40%	10%	$6.00	$15,000
5000	40%	10%	6.50	16,250
4500	40%	10%	6.95	13,500
4000	40%	10%	7.50	15,000
5000	40%	10%	7.50	18,750
6000	40%	10% & 12½%	6.00	17,790

This is scratchwork; probably it is not arranged in a neat table. He wonders whether it would be easier to sell 5000 copies at $6 or 4000 at $7.50, since both produce the same amount of money for publishing expenses—but of course at 5000 copies and $6 there will be the extra cost of producing and handling the additional 1000 copies, so the profit will be less. At any rate, looking at the figures and thinking about the book, the publisher is beginning to get a feel for the market. He glances at the advance copy of the *New York Times Book Review* which has come in the morning mail, noting the prices of several current books in relation to the number of pages, illustrations, type of book, and so forth.

Turning again to the manufacturing estimate, the publisher notes that it is for 5000 and additional 1000s of copies printed at the same time, so he can project the manufacturing cost upward or downward. The manufacturing estimate shows:

	5000	Additional 1000s
Plant cost	$3,580	$ 0
Production cost	4,725	945
Total	$8,305	$ 945

The publisher notices that the unit production cost ($945 divided by 1000) is 94½ cents.

He next wonders whether the income from sales will be sufficient to pay for operating expenses, after the printer's bill has been paid. Using the parameters for operating expenses that have been developed from budget projections, he does the following rough calculations:

A. 352 pages × $6.00 per page	=	$2,100
B. 5000 copies × $.80 per copy	=	4,000
C. General overhead	=	750
D. Advertising budget	=	2,000
Estimated operating cost	=	$8,850

He wonders whether $2000 is enough to allow for out-of-pocket advertising expenses; perhaps it should be higher. Anyway, he can now look at the estimated total cost for a 5000-copy edition:

Manufacturing cost	=	$8,305
Operating cost	=	8,850
Total cost	=	$17,155

Looking again at his arithmetic showing sales revenue (after discount and royalties), he is attracted to the idea of a $7.50 price. After all, like everything else, books are more expensive these days. What does the marketing manager think?

Over the phone the marketing manager reports that he thinks he can sell at least 4000 copies and perhaps 5000 or more in the first year. The editor, however, thinks the author will object to pricing his book over $6.50. The publisher decides in favor of $7.50, but he tells the editor that in view of the marketing manager's enthusiasm, he can offer a royalty advance equivalent to the sale of 4,000 copies; that is, $3000. This is more than the editor expected and he thinks the author will be pleased. (It develops later, however, that the author wants only a $1500 advance, so as to spread his income for tax purposes.)

The publisher is now quite pleased. If he can sell 4000 copies at $7.50 (less discount and royalties) in the first year, he will be only $2000 short of breaking even on a 5000-copy printing, and he estimates that the book will have a continuing sale for several years. His records of sales of similar books show that on the average the second year's sales are 40% of the first year's sales, with the third and fourth years running at 20% and 15% respectively. If the averages hold, and banking on the marketing manager's consecutive estimate of 4000 copies in the first year, the sales pattern should be:

First year	4000 copies
Second year	1600 copies
Third year	800 copies
Fourth year	600 copies
Total for four years	7000 copies

Obviously there will be a good profit if this projection is correct. Even if sales run below the estimate and reach only 6000 copies, there will be a respectable gain. So—the price is to be $7.50, but how many should be printed in the first printing?

The publisher is conscious that his publishing house is short on working capital and he must use it efficiently. It was tempting to try to hold down the advance on royalties on this account, but he is aware that this particular author is sensitive and temperamental, and a generous advance will mean a lot to him (even if he doesn't accept it). Still, the publisher does not want to tie up too much capital in inventory.

He notes again that the unit production cost is 94½ cents, and he knows that he is paying 6½% interest on bank loans and that his costs for warehousing, insurance, etc., are bringing the total carrying charges close to 10%. He finds on the manufacturing estimate that the plant cost of reprinting the book would be $600, and to this he adds $100 for the administrative cost of handling a reprinting, producing a total of $700 for the fixed cost of a reprint. The unit production cost of a reprint should remain about the same.

With these items in hand, he is ready to make a table similar to Table I, calculating carrying charges as average inventory times 94½ cents times 10%, as shown in Table III. Note that the "average of total sale during year" is obtained by adding half of the year's sales to the total sales from preceding years. Thus the average inventory during the year is obtained by subtracting the "average of total sale during year" from the total number printed.

From Table III the publisher can easily see that the optimum number tc print, assuming that his market estimates are reasonably correct and that he has sufficient working capital, is close to 7000 copies. If he wishes he can draw a graph (as shown in Figure 11), though Table III shows clearly that a printing just under 7000 copies will lead to carrying charges of about $700 in the life of the printing.

In fact an experienced publisher will almost certainly not work out either Table III or a graphical solution in detail, though he would have in mind the various considerations that they express. Probably he would decide to print 7000 copies after a brief inspection of cost and market figures and after calculating probable income. Or he might feel that his marketing manager's sales estimates were too optimistic and would hedge his bets by printing 6000 copies, which would also reduce inventory investment and carrying charges, though it would result in reprinting earlier if the market estimates are correct—and if it is decided not to reprint because the sale at that time is too slow, a printing of 6000 copies would result in the loss of the sale of 1000 copies.

Thus having thought through the various matters described in

TABLE III

Year	Yearly sale (copies)	Total sale (copies)	Average of total sale during year (copies)	*Print 5000 copies*			*Print 6000 copies*			*Print 7000 copies*		
				Average inventory (copies)	Yearly carrying charge	Total carrying charge	Average inventory (copies)	Yearly carrying charge	Total carrying charge	Average inventory (copies)	Yearly carrying charge	Total carrying charge
1st	4000	4000	2000	3000	$193	$193	4000	$378	$378	5000	$472	$472
2nd	1600	5600	4800	200	18	211	1200	113	491	2200	197	671
3rd	800	6400	6000				0			1000	94	765
4th	600	7000	6700							300	27	792

the preceding pages, the publisher writes down his publication plan, which is in effect his order to the various departments to proceed as directed. The process as described here seems complicated and involved, but if all the information is at hand, working out a publication plan will perhaps take twenty minutes or even less. The plan itself might be expressed on a printed form, as follows:

PUBLICATION PLAN

Author: Harlan J. Sorenson
Title: THE MEANING OF THE AMERICAN CIVIL WAR
Editor: Robert Dorrance
Trim Size: 5½" x 8½", 352 pages
Manufacturing cost: $10,195 for 7,000 copies
Operating cost: 10,450
Total: $20,645
Price: $7.50, trade discount
Royalty: 10% on first 5,000 copies, 12½% on next 5,000, 15% beyond 10,000
Advance royalty: $1,500
Advertising budget: $2,000
Projected sales income:

6,500 copies x $7.50 x 60%	=	$29,250
Less royalty	=	5,150
Revenue	=	$24,100
Projected profit	=	$ 3,455

Estimated sale: 1st year = 4,000 copies
2nd year = 1,600 copies
3rd year = 800 copies

Similar books:	Copies sold 1st yr	total in __ yrs
1. Abel, THE ORDEAL OF THE SOUTH (1964)	3,625	9,200 in 5
2. Douglas, RAILROADS IN THE CIVIL WAR (1966)	2,850	4,000 in 3

3. Williams, CARPETBAGGERS
IN THE RECONSTRUCTION
(1963) 4,735 11,000 in 6

Subsidiary rights: Possible American History Book Club; try major book clubs but probably not popular enough. Should make a good paperback for school and college use.

Comment: Sorenson's earlier books sold 6,000 copies in 4 years and 15,000 copies in 8 years. Both are now selling well in paperback. We are developing a strong list in American history, and this fits well. See the sales record and pattern of our American history group.

Date: July 12, 1969
Approved: B.P.A.

The plan once approved, with the publisher's initials, is duplicated and sent to the various departments as authorization to proceed. A contract is drawn up and the advance royalty is paid to the author (or his literary agent), the editor works out final revisions with the author, the marketing manager and the designer confer about the art work that will serve as a basis for the jacket and advertising, the production department lets the printer know approximately when the manuscript will be coming and gets a production schedule which is passed to the other departments, and so forth. The publication plan is the framework on which all these other activities hang.

If something happens so that basic changes in the plan are needed—the author wants a section of illustrations requiring a change in format and cost, in the process of revision the author has cut fifty pages from the book, the advance reaction in the bookstores indicates that the print order should be increased, the advertising manager wants a major increase in the advertising budget—the publication plan must be reviewed and changes authorized or rejected. But a carefully prepared publication plan permits everyone to proceed with confidence that the project will work out as expected, that the various aspects are in balance and have been budgeted for, and that the publication of this particular book is an integrated part of the house's publishing program.

Finally, the publication plan provides an opportunity to check prediction against performance. After the book is published, how did the costs compare with the estimates? Did the sales pattern develop as predicted? The comparison of performance with prediction feeds still another item into the experience which the publisher will bring to bear when he makes the decisions that will result in publication plans for future books.

SERIES OF BOOKS

This discussion of micro-publishing, leading up to a publication plan for an individual book, has bypassed the question of series of books, which is a kind of halfway phenomenon between micro-publishing and macro-publishing. In a sense, any publisher's list is a series of books, since a publisher must build up groups of books intended for certain markets. Otherwise he cannot market his books efficiently; it is exceedingly difficult to do a good job of marketing an isolated book in a market for which one has no other books or plans for future books. We have seen that publishers are classified by the markets they serve, which correspond to the types of books they publish, so the books on a publisher's list tend to fall naturally into groups which constitute a kind of series.

Most publishers take advantage of this natural tendency by setting up formal series in areas of interest to them. This has many advantages. One can appoint a distinguished or even famous expert to be the editor of the series, invite other experts to write for the series, to screen manuscripts and advise on revisions, to lend their names and reputations for use in advertising and promotion. The series can be announced publicly, with the name of the editor and the first few titles and authors, thus avoiding the difficulty of entering a new field with a single book. The appearance of a distinguished editor and a few well-known authors as contributors to the series will attract other authors, and a snowball effect may be generated.

All this requires planning and energy; an editor on the house's staff must be assigned to work closely with the outside expert, who has other projects in mind and who may not do very much without house support and stimulation. Usually an overriding royalty is provided for the outside editor, but the main stimulus must be his desire to see the series succeed as a contribution to its field. Royalties to series editors can be substantial, but they build up slowly, and there are many competing demands on the kind of person who makes a good series editor.

There are two main types of series, closed and open-ended. An open-ended series usually has a rather broad subject area, social psychology or nuclear physics, for example, in which one attempts to develop a group of books covering various aspects, more or less according to opportunity, seeking and accepting good manuscripts from many sources, with the idea that the series will grow and continue into the future as long as it is successful. The open-ended series has many advantages. It makes both authors and readers aware of a publisher's continuing interest in a subject area, it provides a framework in which to secure the services of distinguished experts, and it involves little in the way of editorial or financial commitment, since each project or manuscript can be considered on its merits as if it were an individual book. Nevertheless, the publisher of a successful series will tend to accept some books for the series that he would not otherwise accept, to lend distinction to the series, to provide coverage of the field, or to satisfy the editor and encourage him to develop the series further. Moreover, an established series provides a setting in which a book can be successful, even if it would not be successful as an independent publication; it can be carried along by the reputation of the series, libraries will order it to complete their series holdings, bookstores will display it as part of the series, and so forth.

A closed series is a quite different matter. Here one plans a distinct group of books to cover a subject area in a particular way with a definite market in mind. For example, one might plan a series of six books on "Contemporary America," with each book to be written by a well-known expert on some current problem or aspect of American life: the economy, the cities, international affairs, domestic politics, cultural life, and education. One might specify that these books were to be between 250 and 350 pages and were to be written at a senior high school or freshman college level, to be marketed to schools and colleges and also as general trade books. A book club might be sounded out on the possibility of offering the set as a selection or a premium, and foreign rights might be explored. A schedule would be laid out, with deadlines for manuscripts and finished books, and a format would be chosen and costs projected. For such a series it would be important to sign up at least two leading authors in the early stages, so that their names could be used to attract other authors. Probably substantial advances and attractive royalties would be offered. The suggestion for such a series could even come from an author, who would help plan the series and choose the other authors.

A closed series is a definite project with a beginning and an ending, like an individual book. It usually involves more detailed planning and a deeper initial editorial and financial commitment than an open-ended series, but the commitment is limited, the project can be planned and the outcome foreseen with reasonable confidence. Costs and sales can be projected both for individual books and for the series as a whole, and most of the considerations that apply to an individual book can be applied to a closed series.

THE MARKET: MONOPOLY AND COMPETITION

We have emphasized that a book is priced in a market; the publisher considers the book in both its intellectual content and its physical characteristics, and he estimates how many will be sold in a certain period at a certain price. The physical appearance and the number of pages are important because the customer compares this book with other books that *look similar to it.* He doesn't care about the size of the edition or the cost; he wants to buy only one copy of the book and he won't buy it if it's too expensive (though he may get it from a library)—that is, he won't buy it if it seems too expensive when compared with books that look similar. He will expect to pay about the same for a 400-page specialized study of economic aspects of the Civil War (printed in an edition of, say, 2500 copies) as for a 400-page semipopular work on generals and battles in the Civil War. The publisher must recognize this and price his book in the market; as we have seen, there is no formula that will produce a price on the basis of cost.

On the other hand, the publisher has a monopoly on his particular book. He or the author holds the copyright and no one else can publish it. Anyone who wants that particular book must get it from him. If you want a Hemingway novel, you must buy it from Scribner's (or possibly a Scribner's licensee); if you want Samuelson's freshman textbook on economics, you must buy it from McGraw-Hill. This kind of monopolistic situation is qualified by the willingness of readers to read Faulkner instead of Hemingway, for example, or the willingness of teachers to use other textbooks in economics. Thus with strong authors the publishers have some freedom to maximize profits by setting higher prices than a purely competitive situation would indicate, but this freedom is quite limited by the market. In fact it is common in such situations, especially with fiction, to issue several different editions at different prices for different parts of the market: the educational market, the gift-book market, the quality-paperback market, the mass market in drugstores and newsstands. In each of these markets a particular edition will compete with other similar editions of books by other authors.

The publisher's freedom to exercise his monopoly on an individual book by setting a high price is also limited by his relations with authors. Authors, especially those who are not so well established, are anxious not to see their readerships limited by high prices; it is by being read that their reputations are made.

Curiously, the library market seems to be very discount-sensitive, but not very price-sensitive. Libraries tend to order the books they want regardless of price (though they may shop for cheaper editions and bargain with wholesalers over discounts), up to the limits of their budgets. The easy availability of books in free public libaries is another inhibiting factor on book prices.

There is only one Hemingway, only one freshman economics textbook by Samuelson, only one of any title that is issued, but some books are much more "substitutable" than others. Dictionaries, for example, although there are important differences among them, are in fierce price competition because one can easily substitute for another. Moreover, great efforts are made to convince the public of the superiority of one dictionary over another, and many editions of a single basic dictionary will be issued to compete in different markets. Much the same can be said of encyclopedias, though here competition takes a different form because most encyclopedias are sold door-to-door by salesmen, giving a greater opportunity to exploit product differentiation, premium offers, special discounts, personalized service, and the like. Certainly no encyclopedia publisher thinks he is in anything but a highly competitive market.

Not only is the book market highly competitive, but each reader is completely satisfied with only one copy; the publisher cannot sell more copies to the same readers by lowering the price as, for example, more gasoline is sold for the same automobile when the price is lowered. Few people want more than one dictionary or encyclopedia; hardly anyone wants more than one copy of a novel, and once he has read it, he is likely to give it away.

Thus the effect on prices of the publisher's monopoly on an individual book is very small indeed, but the monopoly of copyright does give him certain important advantages. It protects the efforts that he makes to establish a book or an author, and it permits him to profit substantially on some books (where other publishers would otherwise jump in and divide the market) so as to pay for those books that produce losses. That is, the monopoly right permits the publisher to take risks that he would not take if his more successful books were subject to reprinting without permission and without fee. Thus the copyright promotes the public interest by encouraging a great variety of books to be published, many of them economically marginal, in the hope that some will be highly profitable, and it does this without causing significantly higher book prices on account of monopolistic pricing.

As this is written, the United States copyright law is under review and a new law is proposed. This is not the time or place to comment on the proposed new law in detail, but it should be noted that recent court decisions and much of the testimony on the proposed new law, especially from educators, tend to favor free access to published material and a weakening of copyright control. Pressure for free access is reinforced by the prospect of new technologies (see Chapter VI), especially copying technology. Publishers must find better ways of making their publications conveniently available, especially for educational purposes, but it will be unfortunate indeed if the desire of educators and others to gain free access to certain materials causes a weakening of copyright and a consequent reduction of publishers' willingness to risk publication of marginal projects. The result could be culturally retrogressive, since many of the most valuable books, including most first novels and almost all poetry, are in this category.

THE DYNAMICS OF THE MARKET

We have discussed the book market as if it were static, which of course is not the case. The market itself changes in various ways. There are fashions in books—for example, the current fashion for gothic novels or for what Kenneth McCormick, a Doubleday editor, has called "faction." The latter are novels closely based on actual events or institutions, often containing thinly disguised characters from public life. Such fashions are often initiated by a few outstandingly successful books (Drury's *Advise and Consent,* Burdick and Lederer's *The Ugly American*) and are difficult to predict. Other changes, such as the growth of the educational market, can be predicted from population figures or other data. An alert publisher will constantly be watching the world around him, reading the book reviews, studying the American Book Publishers Council's trend figures, listening to authors, browsing in bookstores, reading the daily newspaper and the *Publishers' Weekly,* and trying to anticipate the large and enormously varied book market.

The publisher will also be very conscious of the economics of the market, since he deals with it constantly as he makes decisions on individual books. We have emphasized that no individual publisher can have much impact on the market; he must price his books with reference to the market, to sell in competition with other books of (apparently) similar size and content, and without reference to total cost once the decision to publish has been made. As we have seen, only the variable cost has any effect on the determination of N_{opt} and the optimum list price, and that effect is small compared to that of the estimated demand curve, that is, the market. Yet the publisher is subjected to pressures as his own costs change—the costs of salaries, typesetting, advertising, paper, presswork, binding, and so forth. How can the publisher adjust to changing costs in relation to the market? And how does the market adjust to changing costs?

Since an individual publisher cannot affect the market, he can only adjust to it in the choice of books that he will publish, avoiding those on which he thinks he cannot make a profit or at least break even. Fortunately, from a cultural point of view if not from the publisher's, the market is full of uncertainties. The demand curve is not something that exists as a platonic ideal, to be discerned through philosophic thought; it is the publisher's estimate of what he can sell at various prices, and it exists only in his mind, bordered by a vague penumbra of favorable and unfavorable probabilities. And as we have seen, one publisher's estimate of the demand curve may be different from another's, because of different judgments of the particular book or because one publisher has better marketing facilities and a more appropriate list in a particular field. So there will be variability of decisions on individual books, even while all publishers are faced by essentially the same cost factors. But as cost factors change and as the world changes, the market will gradually change and publishers will respond to it.

This response is most easily seen historically and may be observed by watching the rather hazy boundary between what commercial publishers and nonprofit university presses are publishing. During World War II, when paper was scarce, university students were few, and there was a growing demand for popular books, commercial publishers abandoned large areas of serious nonfiction in favor of more popular titles. An expanding market enabled them to hold prices down, while university presses moved energetically into the publication of serious and sometimes semipopular books of history, politics, science, literary criticism, and so forth.

The expanding market with stable prices continued for some time after the war, while costs were rising, but in the late 'forties publishers began to feel economically pinched, and there was much concern expressed in *Publishers' Weekly* about whether the public would pay more than $3 for a detective story or $5 for a novel. In the early 'fifties publishers began to inch their prices upward, pricing new books higher and repricing old books and reprints. This was not done by any plan, although there was a general awareness of the problem. It was done in detail as individual publishers responded to their desires to stay in business and to continue to publish certain kinds of books, and as they saw the public gradually adjusting to a new price level. This movement has continued into the heavily inflationary period of the 'sixties, while general prosperity has enabled a sufficient public to buy some very expensive books, for example, lavishly illustrated art books at $25 to $50 or more.

Meanwhile the boundary between commercial and university publishers had been changing, as the cost-price relationships changed and as colleges and graduate schools expanded. For example, in the late 'forties there was only a small market for advanced books in political theory and in the more specialized areas of higher mathematics. University presses had these fields to themselves, and some established strong lists of important books, published at high cost in small editions, usually with the expectation of financial loss. But as time passed and prices rose while graduate schools expanded, these areas became increasingly attractive to commercial publishers, who began to reclaim areas that they had abandoned, while the university presses, already established in these areas, extended their efforts to even more specialized books that could now find a place in the expanded market.

The development of the so-called quality-paperback market in the 'fifties is another example of the dynamic adjustment of prices, costs, and public demand. The adjustment to higher prices in the 'fifties was felt especially by students. Meanwhile the technology of "perfect" (or glued) binding had been improved, with new machines and new adhesives for binding books cheaply. In 1953 a press at the Doubleday printing plant was underutilized, and Jason Epstein, then a Doubleday editor, only recently a student himself, saw an opportunity to reissue books of intellectual importance at prices that students could afford. He persuaded the officers of Doubleday, and the first series of Anchor Books was issued. The response of the public, and especially of students and professors, shows that an unfulfilled demand had existed, and a new submarket within the larger market for books was created. This would probably not have been possible in the late 'forties, but conditions in 1953 were favorable, resulting in a change in the market that promises to be enduring. Meanwhile rising costs have been gradually forcing paperback prices upward, and as this has happened, university presses have been able to utilize the paperback market to get wider distribution of some of their specialized books, at the same time reclaiming some of their more popular titles that had formerly been leased to commercial publishers.

Thus the market changes, responding to many factors within and beyond the publishing industry. Though the market is sluggish in its response, costs must ultimately have their influence, even though cost is an indirect factor in the pricing of any individual book. Thus thousands of micro-publishing decisions have their cumulative effect, not only on the fate of individual publishing houses but on the book market as a whole.

V

PLANNING

In a sense, planning is synonymous with management. Management is control, and the daily work of management is to make decisions that will control the future. Decisions are made in the framework of policies that have continuing force—and the slower development of policies is also a kind of planning.

If planning is making decisions now in order to achieve future effects, the regular work of the several departments of a publishing house includes large amounts of planning, mostly short-range planning. The editorial department searches for manuscripts that will often not be published for at least a year, and the editors hope to find authors who will produce for the house for many years. The designers plan the appearance of future books. The production department plans schedules and buys materials for future use. The marketing department plans its advertising schedules and sales programs. The accounting department projects future cash flow. And so forth.

In short, managers at all levels are engaged in looking ahead. At the departmental level, managers plan for the relatively short range, rarely more than a year. Such plans are usually in the form of the schedules, frequently revised, that are the everyday tools for laying out work and for communication within the house.

The marketing department watches the production schedule to keep track of plans for books they have worked on. The development, discussion, circulation, and criticism of such plans is part of the internal activity that coordinates and improves the functioning of the several departments. The operating budget is the prime example of such a short-term plan, since making a budget requires all the departments to look ahead, and the budget, once adopted, is at the same time a goal and a restriction, subject to frequent review and revision.

If we think of short-range planning as being limited to not more than a year, then most short-range planning is done at the departmental level and is reviewed interdepartmentally in various ways by various committees, often composed of department heads, and is approved at least in general at a higher level of management. Often such approval is in the form of budget adoption.

At higher levels the management must plan for the longer range, perhaps three to five or even more years, and long-range plans inevitably involve the house as a whole, including the coordinated development of all departments. Except for the budget, virtually all planning for the house as a whole is long-range planning and is carried out by the top management and approved by the board of directors. The board of directors (or final authority, however the house is organized) must be involved because long-range planning vitally affects the future of the house and can determine its ultimate success or failure. The board must know where the house stands and where it is going, and it must check its progress toward specified goals.

This again raises the question of objectives, which was discussed in Chapter I. What to plan for? What are the long-range goals and intermediate objectives? What kind of long-range plans will help realize those goals?

Most commercial publishers can express long-range goals in terms of profitability and growth—that the profit should be maintained at a certain percent of assets and that assets should increase by a certain percent per year. Underneath such numerical goals is the usual assumption that the house will stay in the book publishing business (that is, it will not expand by going into the toy business, for example), but it is not stated whether the house will expand into new areas of publishing. Should the required growth be achieved by expanding sales through expanding markets in fields of present operation, by publishing more books in present fields, or by going into new fields? How will such expansion be staffed and financed? Will such expansion require internal reorganization or the establishment of new divisions, branch offices, or remote warehouse and service operations? Will new physical facilities be needed?

To be more specific, an adult trade publisher might consider whether to establish its own paperback line, whether to go into college text or el-hi (elementary and high school) publishing, whether to publish juveniles, and so forth. A special problem has arisen with educational publishers, particularly those that have been purchased by electronics companies, since they increasingly tend to regard themselves as in "the knowledge industry" rather than "the book industry," and this leads them into nonbook activities of various kinds—film strips, motion pictures, computer-aided instruction, tapes and records, television and radio, and other educational devices. This is probably a healthy change, but it greatly complicates the problem of long-range planning, especially for executives who have grown up in book publishing. The knowledge industry includes most book publishing and the conception of a unified and coordinated knowledge industry may lead to improvements in education at all levels and may change the tastes of the adult population. If so, long-range planning for all book publishers will have to be done in the context of the knowledge industry, since planning must be done in relation to markets.

Even publishers who cannot state their long-range goals in terms of percentages of profitability and growth, such as a church-sponsored religious publisher or a university press, must plan in relation to markets. What markets can be reached with the religious message the house wants to propagate, and by what forms of publishing can they be reached most effectively? Should the house sponsor trade juveniles with a religious message or should it stick to Sunday-school texts? Or, for a university press, what are the long-range requirements for research publications in economics? in literary history and criticism? in biology? And how can the press serve them best? Should the press establish a new series in microbiology or comparative literature? Should it publish bibliographies, or new editions of classic works? Such questions, which are the essence of long-range planning, inevitably involve markets—that is, readers—just as much as the long-range plans of profit-oriented publishers do. And such questions for nonprofit publishers raise the same or perhaps even more acute problems of personnel development and financing, since the nature of a nonprofit publisher's purpose limits its ability to finance its own expansion.

On the other hand, the chartered purpose of a nonprofit publishing house to a large extent determines the general nature of its long-range goals and simplifies and limits its long-range planning to that extent. A university press, for example, will plan for publication of scholarly and scientific research; it does not need to consider whether to establish a division for juveniles. And although a university press must plan in terms of markets, we saw in Chapter II that for professional publishing the readers and the authors were part of the same group, so that planning in terms of markets and editorial planning are virtually the same thing. University presses and other publishers of professional books can plan largely in terms of the needs of professional authors to disseminate what they have to say, on the assumption that the professionals who need the information will constitute a market.

In general, however, publishers must expand through the growth of present markets and the development and establishment of new markets. New-product development, which can be a major source of growth for industrial companies, is severely limited for book publishers, except in the sense that each new book or series is a new product. Occasionally a new field of publishing that is the equivalent of a new product will emerge, as trade paperback publishing did in the 'fifties. More will be said on this subject in the discussion of new technologies. But so far as books in the usual sense are concerned, the publisher must survey and project the markets and must plan in terms of future markets.

Readers are individual, but markets are categorized and institutionalized. Educational institutions are the largest single market for books, and the graduates of schools and colleges are tomorrow's readers as well as today's. At least, tomorrow's readers will come from the ranks of the graduates of schools and colleges, though unfortunately the number of regular book readers is only a small proportion of the graduates. Still, the statistics of school and college population, year by year, are the prime indicators of future markets. The United States Office of Education publishes such figures, and they are collected and presented for the book industry by the American Book Publishers Council and the American Educational Publishers Institute.

Although the population of educational institutions is a prime indicator for future book markets, it must be interpreted in detail for different types of books; the projection for medical or other professional books would be different from that for juveniles. Also, the amounts of money available for the purchase of books will not be in strict proportion to the population. Again, a medical student will spend far more for books than the average college student. Government programs supporting public education can make enormous differences in expenditures for books, and these can be specific with respect to books at different levels and on different subject areas. Thus a publisher's long-range plans will probably be affected by his assessments of specific trends in education at various levels, the probable expenditures in various areas of education, and his judgment of his ability to serve that market in competition with other publishers.

Public libraries and school and college libraries constitute another major segment of the market that may affect long-range planning. Statistics on library expenditures for books are published in the *Bowker Annual of Library and Book Trade Information* and they must also be interpreted specifically by type of library in relation to type of book. A very large proportion (no one knows just how large, but perhaps fifty percent) of hardbound books (excluding textbooks) are sold eventually to libraries either directly by publishers or through dealers. Projected library expenditures should be an element of long-range planning, though this is difficult to estimate because library budgets are very sensitive to the state of the economy generally, the vagaries and variations of local taxes, and the uncertainties of congressional support for national programs. Much the same could be said of expenditures for books in public schools, but students must have textbooks, and library budgets are cut first. Thus statistics on the educational population, while essential for estimating textbook sales, are not so useful in estimating future sales to school libraries. The libraries buy general books and reference books, and their purchases can change markedly from year to year.

The most visible part of the book market is the general book-reading public, the ill-defined and amorphous group of people who go to bookstores to buy books for recreational reading or for information and self-improvement. The size of this market in terms of numbers of readers is unknown; probably it is proportional to the number of high school and college graduates in the population. Its size in terms of expenditures can be estimated by projecting the annual trend reports of the American Book Publishers Council, and it can be described geographically by examination of regional sales experience. In this market a large proportion of sales are sought by publicity, supplemented by advertising, in the hope of stimulating public discussion and creating a best-seller psychology—"Everybody's reading it." Gift sales and impulse sales from bookstore displays are also important, especially before Christmas. Consequently this is a very unreliable and fickle market, difficult to plan for.

Many books in the adult trade field are published at a loss or a modest profit in the hope of generating a few that will be widely popular. Among Harper & Row's list of its thirty most profitable titles for 1968, there were only five adult trade books, and the profit from these included substantial sums in subsidiary rights. (The rest of the thirty could be categorized as follows: ten college texts, ten el-hi texts, two reference works, one juvenile, one medical, and one religious.) Moreover, all five of the most profitable adult trade books were published in 1967, while in other categories nineteen titles (76%) were originally published in 1965 or earlier and will probably continue to be highly profitable in future years. Thus one sees that adult trade publishing is highly speculative, with large returns from a few titles and small returns on many, and even the successes usually have a rather short life. Long-range planning is therefore exceedingly difficult except in general terms such as the number of books to be published, the amount of money to be invested, and the size of the staff that will be needed. The entire operation will have to be flexible, and the editors must sense popular tastes, anticipate public interest in a variety of subjects and events, cultivate authors who seem to have the potential to reach wide readerships, capitalize on unforeseen opportunities, and not go overboard on too many unsuccessful projects.

If a commercial house defines its objectives in terms of percentages of profit and growth, it must first assess whether its goals are achievable in the field of publishing in which it now operates. Are the markets growing fast enough? Can it enlarge its share of the market? Can it find or reach new markets—that is, reach new readers and help the market grow? Within its own field of publishing, can it finance the desired growth—that is, can it generate sufficient profits to provide an adequate return for shareholders or owners and still have enough money to invest in growth, since more working capital will be needed for a larger operation? If more working capital is needed, should it be obtained by issuing shares or by borrowing? Should it be short- or long-term borrowing, and what interest will be required?

If the house feels that it wants to go into new fields of publishing, even more money will be required. Entering a new field will require new personnel and probably a new department or other subunit of the organization. Time will be needed to establish the new activity, and substantial expenses will be incurred before any books are published. Thus, after assessing the markets, the house will have to examine financial implications even more carefully. Perhaps the long-range plans will have to be trimmed to adjust to financial capabilities, but markets themselves are demanding, and it is difficult for a house to hold back and control its growth when markets are expanding. This is a primary cause of many mergers and stock issues of publishing houses in the 'sixties; working capital simply could not be generated fast enough to meet the requirements of the expanding markets.

In planning for major expansion, the publisher must do what the banker does; he must examine his own balance sheet to determine the house's financial health now, and even more important, he must project the effect on the balance sheet of whatever new financing is required. What will the various test ratios be *after* the financing has taken place? Will the house still be financially sound? Will income be sufficient to repay loans and pay dividends as required? Will the control of the house be affected, and if so, how? What will be the effects of possible new factors in control? What would be the effects of restraining growth to avoid the dangers of overexpansion?

The result of all these deliberations should be a long-range plan, beginning with a set of goals for perhaps five years ahead. In order to achieve coordination of its several aspects, the plan should be explicit, in written form, not just a series of entries in the minutes of various meetings of the board of directors. It should state the objectives and the general approaches to them. It should envision personnel expansion and reorganization on a phased schedule, with editorial, design, production, marketing, and accounting staff added in time for training so that they will be ready when they are needed. It should take account of new management requirements, and from all these projections it should show a schedule of future operating expenses. At the same time it will be necessary to estimate future investment in production and future sales in order to foresee the growth of inventory and receivables.

In short, a long-range plan will outline the projected future operations with respect to personnel, production, and sales; and it will show estimated results in terms of the operating statement and balance sheet. It will reveal the need for working capital, and will include the means of financing projected growth. It should be realistic but conservative, and it should envision contingent actions if the results are either better or worse than expected. If the new plan does not go well, will it be possible to pull out, or will the commitment be too heavy? If it goes very well, can it be expanded faster? Is the projected timing fast enough to permit sufficient impact to ensure success? It is hard to enter a new market with just a few books. Is the schedule so fast that new personnel will be swamped before they have a chance to get properly organized? What will be the effects of new activities on older parts of the house's program?

Just as the annual budget is a kind of short-range plan, the long-range plan is a kind of budget, anticipating the interaction of operating and financial aspects. Like a budget it must be reviewed periodically and revised in accordance with actual performance and perhaps with modified objectives. A five-year plan, for example, can be accelerated or retarded after the first year, and possibly its goals will be revised in the light of experience. The plan may be extended another year into the future and adopted as a new five-year plan. Thus long-range planning keeps working ahead into the future, providing a framework for current activities and giving confidence in the success of major long-term projects.

THE EFFECTS OF NEW TECHNOLOGIES

Up to this point, my remarks on planning have assumed that the publishing industry will continue to expand in much the same way and with much the same structure that now exists. But there has been much speculation, some of it rather rash, on the effects of new technologies on book publishing, and the mergers of publishing houses with electronics corporations have provided a basis for such speculation. Will there be fundamental changes in the book-publishing industry, and how can long-range planning take account of such changes? The technologies themselves will be further discussed in Chapter VI, but here we will attempt to put them in general categories with respect to planning.

First, it is important to realize that technological changes have been occurring at an increasingly rapid rate for at least the past twenty years. Photocomposition has evolved so that now it is a widely used technique. The photo-offset process has been enormously improved, with much better plates, capable of taking very fine screens and producing a very black image. Special varieties such as dry offset and deep-etch offset have become available. Inks and paper have been improved. Newly designed presses run faster and produce better impressions, and web presses are becoming increasingly economical even for short runs. Color printing is becoming better and relatively less expensive as electronic color analyzers and printing methods are improved. New thermoplastic and other adhesives have been invented for binding, machines for adhesive binding have been invented, and conventional binding machinery and methods have been improved. One of the tasks of today's production manager is to keep informed about the steady flow of new devices and materials and techniques that are available and coming into use by book printers. These technological changes enable him to produce books of higher quality more cheaply and more rapidly.

But what they are producing is still the conventional book,

presumably to be distributed to the reader in the conventional way. Changes of the kind that have been going on for the past twenty years can be accommodated by and are welcomed by publishers in the normal course of development, and such changes will no doubt continue in the future. Let us, as an exercise, imagine one of the most radical developments that could occur in the technology of book production within the conventional framework: the invention of economical means for the production of letterpress-quality copies of books in single-copy editions. In fact, this has already happened (though not yet up to letterpress quality) and is being used by such firms as University Microfilms, a subsidiary of Xerox Corporation, to produce copies of out-of-print books as needed. One must have a single copy to start with, from which copies will be made, or one might have a magnetic tape on which the book would exist in code, to be reproduced by some kind of superspeed photo-printer. The present devices are not quite up to competition with conventional printing, either in quality or price, but they are getting closer, especially for small editions. How will publishing be affected when the single-copy edition becomes competitive, and how can this be anticipated in long-range planning?

To estimate the effects, let us look back to Chapter IV on micro-publishing, where we saw in Figure 21 that the manufacturing cost consisted of a fixed plant cost plus a production cost proportional to the number of copies printed. One can easily see that Figure 21 also shows the graph of manufacturing cost for books produced in single-copy editions, since the cost of producing the first copy or the magnetic tape would be the plant cost and the cost of producing additional single copies would be the unit production cost. The publisher would still have to estimate sales at various possible prices in order to decide how to price the book and how expected income would relate to costs. The major difference would be that he would not have to decide how many to print, since just enough copies of each title on his list would be printed each day to fill that day's orders. Thus his warehousing costs would be virtually eliminated, as would his write-off costs, since he would have no inventory to write off. As we saw on the typical operating statements in Chapter III, shipping and warehousing usually runs about 5%, and write-offs run around 2% of net receipts. Other operating costs would remain the same. Shipping facilities would still be needed, so perhaps the total saving in a single-copy-edition operation would be 4% or 5%. This would be a welcome saving, but it would hardly require a radical reorganization of the publishing house.

The change in the balance sheet of a single-copy-edition operation would be much more important, since the inventories would be eliminated, and the amount of working capital needed to sustain a given sales level would be greatly reduced. The risk of publishing new books would be somewhat reduced, and this should encourage experimental publishing. Thus the house should become relatively much more profitable, more because of reduction of investment than because of reductions in cost. In planning a change from conventional to single-copy-edition operation, as many houses surely will when the technology becomes economical, the house will liquidate its inventory over several years, issuing new books and reprinting old ones by the single-copy process. The kind of thinking required to determine print orders by the edition-printing process, as described in Chapter IV, will tend to become obsolete, though I believe it will be many years before single-copy printing can compete in cost for books that sell in large editions, such as textbooks and Bibles. Nor will single-copy editions soon be able to meet the kind of fast demand that is necessary for popular best sellers. Thus the evolution will be gradual, as publishers first switch their reprinting to single-copy editions, then their slower moving new books that would be done in small editions anyway, and later most books except those needed in really large editions or needed quickly in large quantities to meet popular demand.

A shift to single-copy-edition publishing might at first seem rather radical, but apparently it would not be. In the next chapter we will estimate the effects of other new technologies on publishing, technologies that may affect the basic structure of the industry. I shall not attempt to say how publishers can plan for such changes except to indicate that the kinds of changes that are envisioned cannot take place very rapidly, so a publisher who is thinking in long-range terms should be able to anticipate and adjust as changes occur. The rate of introduction of television in the 'forties and 'fifties is perhaps a measure of the speed at which similar new technical innovations can be introduced. Television did not put radio or motion pictures out of business, nor did it reduce book reading, as many feared. It had other good and some very bad cultural effects, and like most of the new devices now envisioned, it offered a new medium for the promotion of books and for the presentation of the material contained in books.

VI

THE NEW TECHNOLOGIES

THERE HAS BEEN MUCH wild speculation about the effects on publishing of new technologies, especially computer technology. Some recent articles would make one think that the book of the future will emerge untouched by human hands, without author or publisher, produced miraculously by an electronic computer guided only by a mysterious person called a programmer. When we reach the millennium in which we are all fitted with electrodes on our heads, with suitable connections to our brains (like rats that I have seen in laboratories), even readers will not be necessary. We will just plug in, and the computer will do the rest. Lord help us when there is a short circuit!

A much more sober approach would be to look at technologies that are actually in existence or now under development and at devices and systems which are either possible or probable within the next twenty-five years.

But, first, there are a number of functions that the new technologies will not perform. Clearly, they will not replace the author, laboring alone over problems of thought and expression. They will not remove the need for editorial judgment and selection, though they may ease such problems by permitting inexpensive trial runs. They will not replace publishing initiative or effective sales and promotion. They will not make the book obsolete, though they may change its form greatly, and some types of books may become obsolete.

But let us begin with something simple, something that is here now, the effects of which have only begun to be seen, namely, copying machines. Such devices are now in offices and libraries everywhere, widely used without regard to copyright, and the trend is just beginning. The more elaborate, automatic copying machines rival printing presses; the simpler ones are improving and becoming less expensive. Home copiers are becoming widespread. It will soon be as common to have a personal copying machine as a tape recorder. Do-it-yourselfers will build their own from kits provided by alert manufacturers, and it will be as impossible to control copying as it is to control the taping of broadcasts. People will duplicate things that they like, building personal libraries of copied material, just as they now build collections of tape recordings. They will make copies for friends, and there will be copies of copies.

Libraries have only begun to realize the potential of copying machines. Since photocopies will soon be produced at less cost than acquiring original books, there will be no need for any well-equipped and well-organized library to have more than one copy of any book. Nor will there be any need to maintain the costly apparatus of general circulation; it will be cheaper to provide a library user with his own copy of whatever he wants, and no book will ever go out of the librarian's direct control—a librarian's dream! Some libraries now follow this practice with scholarly and scientific journals. The library itself may largely take the form of microcards or microfiche, arranged for easy projection and copying.

A scholar recently told me that he had canceled all his subscriptions to scholarly journals. They were taking up too much shelf space, and he found that it is easier and cheaper to scan the tables of contents in the library and get photocopies of only those articles that interest him. He is building a personal reference library in the form of copies of articles in file drawers. Of course, this scholar is not paying for the articles, he is paying only for the copying; and if all scholars followed his practice, there would be no scholarly journals. In fact, there are periodicals which simply publish the tables of contents of scholarly and scientific journals, from which one can order (or copy) the particular articles one wants.

The development of cheap copiers is just the beginning. Using the copying technology, we can expect remote copying to follow shortly. A book or article will be inserted in a machine in New York and a copy will be produced in Chicago or California, transmitted over a network of wires connecting all major libraries and perhaps bookstores. Think what a boon to libraries this would be—instant interlibrary loan from a single complete collection, perhaps the Library of Congress. Only one copy of each book would be needed for national library use, and the enormous expense of repeated cataloguing and shelving would be saved. Perhaps, to conserve space, the single copy in the national central library would be in microfilm, for reproduction on demand only.

The combination of the computer with remote copying technology will make some types of publications obsolete, such as scholarly journals, symposia, and certain kinds of reference works. It will be necessary to publish only the indexes, perhaps with summaries or digests, and the wanted article can be transmitted on demand from a central station. The computer-based master index of biological journals, issued by the Biological Sciences Information Services of Biological Abstracts, could serve as the foundation for such a system. The Clearinghouse for Federal Scientific and Technical Information provides a similar system for scientific reports produced with government support. The Committee for Scientific and Technical Information of the Federal Council for Science and Technology has recommended establishment of a national Scientific and Technical Information Bureau to handle all S&T information; this would eventually be under a national library administration, of which the Library of Congress would be a part. Once such a system is set up for science, its apparatus can be used for all kinds of publications. It is not irrelevant here to note that the *Wall Street Journal* and *Time* are regularly transmitted by wire from a central office for remote printing, and recently several paperback books (the Warren Commission report, for example) have been teletyped from New York to Chicago for rapid production. Of course, these are instances of mass production rather than on-demand publication.

The next logical step is the production of printed materials in the home by remote copiers, using signals from central locations. Newspapers and perhaps magazines will be produced this way, and possibly some books of mass appeal. Although most will probably not be suitable for this kind of distribution, with rising educational levels it may eventually become an important medium even for books. Such remote copiers for home use will likely not be much more complex or expensive than television sets. In fact, it is conceivable that the remote home copier may be simply an attachment to the television set of the future, producing the morning newspaper in the home, on schedule, with as little time lag as television news.

Most of the technology for such devices exists, and one can expect engineering development to take place where there is a commercial incentive. This, for the time being, is coming not from the book industry but from the copying, the electronic, and the news and magazine industries. Once these devices and systems exist, however, the book industry will be profoundly affected, and publishers will adapt and use them.

This is not the place for a detailed discussion of the actual technologies, but it may be pertinent to indicate that the new systems will probably still originate in keyboarding, the equivalent of typesetting, in order to produce the image that is to be reproduced and copied. However, there has been much progress on photoelectric readers that can replace the human eye and hand when dealing with edited manuscripts. From that point, new but already familiar processes will take over—magnetic tape, computers, transmission devices, cathode-ray and laser beams, and image-transfer devices. Research is needed to perfect these devices and make them economical, but most of them are further developed than television was twenty years ago, and the rate of advancement now is much faster. As the technologies are perfected, the structure of book publishing will change.

The new technologies make it clear that what a publisher sells is not a book but the image of a book. The author writes the manuscript; then the publisher selects it for publication, edits it, and gives it a suitable typographic dress—an image. Currently he sells this image as printed on paper and bound in cloth or paper at a single manufacturing establishment; in the future he will usually sell the image as reproduced on copying machines at many locations, by remote or local control, on demand. Forward-looking publishers should begin now to develop systems that will allow them to maintain control over the image that they and the author have produced, requiring payment that will recompense both author and publisher, providing incentive for further effort.

The payments for permission to copy may well become the largest part of a publisher's income, and unless the publisher can control the image and receive appropriate payment, he will go out of business. Thus it is essential to provide means, under a firm copyright law, to service requests for copying permission efficiently and quickly, and at appropriate fees. Otherwise the book image, so easily stolen, will be lost altogether.

Vital cultural interests and large commercial interests are at stake. The new machines will be invented and they will be used. Cheap copiers will be available in many homes, and it will be as futile to attempt to control them as to control the use of home tape-recording machines today. But there is no need to permit free replication of multiple copies for sale or for classroom use, any more than sale of a home recording of a symphony broadcast would be permitted today.

The best hope for authors and publishers is to join the technological revolution. They must devise ways to make it easy for users to obtain permission to make copies for reasonable fees, and they must clearly indicate what kinds of copying are permitted without charge. Only if this is done can publishers insist on compliance with the law or prosecute illegal copiers.

Today all requests for permission to make copies (or to reprint) are handled individually by publishers. A teacher wishing to put together a selection of readings for a class must write to a dozen publishers, one or two of which may not reply promptly, and widely varying payments may be required. The easy thing for the teacher to do is to ignore the law, make the copies, and say to himself, "It really doesn't matter—my class is so small, and after all, the library *bought* the books I'm copying." But the teacher never thinks that he is cheating the author and publisher of a rightful payment, however small, and that this occurrence may be multiplied hundreds of thousands of times throughout the nation.

To meet the teacher's need, the publishers could establish a computer-based central clearinghouse from which anyone could obtain a batch of permissions quickly by making one phone call or sending one letter. If a publisher can write down a permissions policy and rate for each title, taking into account various types of use, such information can be punched onto cards or stored in a computer's memory. With this information, the clearinghouse for permissions could quickly give an answer to a question, authorize copying, send a bill, and collect payments for authors and publishers. Major requests (to reprint a whole book, for example) could be referred to the original publishers, but the bulk of applications could be handled simply and automatically, and there would be little excuse for making multiple copies illegally. I do not say that it would be easy to plan such a clearinghouse. There would be many problems, including the question of expense, but if the incentive to write and publish is to be maintained and private literary property is to be recognized and protected, some such system will be necessary. The adoption of Standard Book Numbering in England and the United States is a step in the right direction, since a computerized clearinghouse could be based on it.

Everything I have said above applies equally to remote copying, which would in fact be easier to control because responsible public institutions such as schools and libraries, which could be counted on to respect the law, would be the chief users. A national central library issuing copies by wire or a local library producing a copy for a "borrower" could be expected to record the event and make appropriate payment. Identification and counting devices attached to copying machines could provide an automatic log of copying activity.

The effects of the technological revolution are already being seen in the recent merging of publishing houses with electronics corporations (Random House with RCA, Wesleyan University Press with Xerox, Holt, Rinehart, and Winston with CBS, and Science Research Associates with IBM, for example). The stage is being set for further development. Although local copiers will become cheaper, as television sets have, the central equipment and network facilities of the transformed industry will be enormously expensive, requiring capital outlay far beyond the resources of any but the largest book publishers.

Thus the trend to merge will continue as far as the Department of Justice will let it, perhaps resulting in only a few large publication networks, as is the case in radio and television. The Random House–RCA merger even suggests that the publishing networks may partly coincide with the present radio-TV systems, using many of the same research and transmission facilities. Small publishers will have to struggle to fit into this structure, finding specialized nooks not occupied by the giants, renting time on the national networks, or being incorporated into larger systems. There may even have to be some federal regulation, as with the radio-TV networks and the public utilities, to insure freedom of expression in the public interest. The printed word has for centuries been the resort of unpopular opinions, but if the distribution of the printed word becomes monolithic owing to technical developments (I hesitate to call it progress), some public guarantee of access may be required. Let us hope that publishing will never reach this state.

Nothing in what I have suggested indicates that the book will become obsolete, though at first glance this might seem to be the case. The book cannot become obsolete any more than the poem or the novel can become obsolete, because the book, though in not quite the same sense as a poem or a novel, is an intellectual construct; it embodies thought and expression beyond a certain indefinite minimum length, and as long as men think and express themselves in writing, books will be written and published. A novelist or a scholar writes a book partly to crystallize his own thought and feeling; cultural progress depends on the dissemination of such writings, which are books.

Nor can the book reader, the man sitting in a chair late at night totally absorbed in the bound volume in his hand, become obsolete, and he is as essential to the writer as the book is to him. The book is the medium, and the publisher is the agent who encourages (and pays) the author and who turns the manuscript into a booklike image, makes it known and wanted, and transmits it to the reader. All the technologies I have described have to do with the transmission of books.

Technologies have their own force and logic, and we have seen how the great promise of television has led us to a wasteland, where the few worthwhile programs are engulfed in trivia and pap. There is danger that the new technologies will have something like the same effect on books. We must be sure that the structure and economics of book publishing in the future are not such as to drive out quality in a kind of electronic Gresham's Law. I, for one, am confident that with intelligence and planning the new technologies *can* be used to make good books as ubiquitous as television, to our great cultural benefit.

EPILOGUE: ON QUALITY

A PUBLISHER IS KNOWN not by the skill with which he runs his business but by the books he publishes. The history of publishing is the history of great houses that published great books; it is also the history of literary taste, which itself is made in part by publishers. The purpose of the activity we have been analyzing is to produce and distribute books, and it is worthwhile only to the extent that the books are worthwhile—and only to the extent that they are read.

It has been said that printing, like architecture, is a servant art. Printing serves publishing, and publishing serves civilization. Books reach every aspect of our culture, interpreting the past and the present, anticipating the future, carrying necessary information, portraying life as it was and is and as it can be imagined. All kinds of books do this, and all kinds of publishers have opportunities to exercise judgment on quality—on the effects of what they publish, for books *do* have effects, both good and bad. If a publisher runs his business well, he has greater opportunities to favor quality, to distribute it widely, and thus to contribute something worthwhile to mankind.

APPENDIX:
SOME USEFUL FORMS

Forms are a means for convenient standardized communication. They can be enormously useful, or they can proliferate in an office until they take more time than they save or cause confusion by errors that occur in unnecessary duplication of information. It is a helpful exercise in a publishing house to collect and review all forms in use. Each department should review its own forms, and an interdepartmental review should be conducted by department heads, since many forms are used to convey information from one department to another. Each publishing house will need to develop its own forms; the following list simply indicates some that may be useful, indicating what sort of information is contained on each. The forms are categorized by source; the recipients are designated or are in most cases obvious. Standard forms such as invoices are not included.

I. *General Administration*

1. *Publishing schedule,* arranged chronologically. Month, author, title, price, discount, quantity.
2. *Change of title, price, or discount notice.* Must be approved by the publisher or authorized staff. Includes a distribution list of staff who must know such changes immediately. The form must also indicate the effective date of change.
3. *Publication plan* (see page 162).

4. *Author contract form.* There are many variations in author contract forms. Each publisher must work out his own form with his legal counsel. The usual parts of the contract are:

a) date, and names of the parties to the contract.

b) author's grant. The most complete grant would be full and exclusive rights during the term of copyright and renewals to publish or to cause others to publish the work in all forms and in all languages throughout the world. Many contracts restrict the grant in various ways—with respect to area, language, or form (motion picture rights, etc.).

c) author's warranty. The author affirms that he controls the rights which he grants, and that the work is not a plagiarism and does not contain obscene or libelous matter.

d) publisher's agreement to publish. When the contract is made in advance, for an unfinished or projected manuscript, this paragraph usually contains an escape clause, requiring the manuscript to conform to certain standards, which are often quite vague.

e) protection of sale. The author agrees not to write a competing book.

f) delivery of manuscript. Specifies the date of delivery (after which the contract is void) and the form of the manuscript (typewritten, double-spaced, etc.). This paragraph may also specify terms regarding illustrations (including permissions) and preparation of the index, if any.

g) author's alterations. The cost of alterations in proof, beyond a certain amount, is usually charged to the author.

h) revised editions. The author agrees to revise when requested or to permit others to revise. This is especially important in textbook contracts.

i) insurance. The publisher agrees to insure the manuscript, illustrations, photos, etc., up to a certain amount.

j) royalties. The royalty periods (usually six-month intervals) and dates of payment are specified. Also the percentage rate (of list or net price), often increasing as more copies are sold. Many special situations are covered: foreign sales, special discounts over a certain percentage, royalty-free copies, paperbacks or cheap editions, and others.

k) other rights. Specifies the division of income from subsidiary rights: translation, first and second serial rights (before and after publication), abridgment, paperback, condensation, digest, adaptation, syndication, omnibus volumes, receipts from licenses to publish; the author's share of income from these rights is usually 50%. The author retains a larger share of income from licenses for dramatization, public reading, radio, motion pictures, television, and reproduction in sight or sound by mechanical devices, usually 85%.

l) termination clause. The rights usually revert to the author if, on request, the publisher fails to keep the work in print. The author may then have the right to purchase the plates, if any, at some proportion of cost.

m) option clause. The author agrees to offer the publisher his next book or sometimes several books.

n) additional provisions. A blank space in the form for the inclusion of special terms.

o) assignment. The agreement is usually binding on heirs and assigns, nor can it be assigned without the consent of both parties.

p) signatures, usually with witnesses.

II. *Editorial Department*

1. *Manuscript acknowledgment form.*
2. *Manuscript registration record.* Author, title, date received, number of pages, number of illustrations, editors or readers consulted and fees paid, final disposition and date.
3. *Staff reader's report.* Brief description of book. Information about author. Names and credentials of outside consultants. Evaluation of book. Market and price estimates. Preliminary recommendation.
4. *Outside reader's confidential report.* This is a report from an expert or a consultant and the questions on the form will depend on the type of manuscript or type of publishing house. Outside readers are usually asked about content (accuracy, style, suitability for course use, etc.) but they are not usually asked about the size of the market, which the publisher should be able to estimate better.
5. *Editor's monthly report* to chief editor on manuscripts under consideration. Date received, author, title, brief status report, from each staff editor.
6. *Author's information for sales promotion* (to be returned with signed contract). Name, book title, address, place and date of birth, citizenship, education and professional training, career (dates and titles), travels, honors, published works, suggestions for review copies, suggestions for publicity copies, suggestions for direct mail (lists),

other promotion suggestions, a brief description of the book for promotional purposes, photograph of author.

7. *Chief copyeditor's editorial work schedule.* Author, title, editor, designer, date manuscript submitted, date to copyeditor, number of manuscript pages, scheduled and actual date to design department. Copies to design department and production department.

8. *Copyeditor's manuscript report* (submitted to chief copyeditor with edited manuscript). Title, author, series, date when final revised manuscript received from author, date copyediting completed, material still to come, number of manuscript pages, number of estimated printed pages (indicate if printer's estimate available), number of illustrations (linecuts, halftones, other), number of proofs needed, author's address.

9. *Editor's promotion suggestions* (to marketing department). Free copy obligations (author, indexer, etc.) and publicity copies, subject category, level of appeal, style, selling line (twenty-five words or less), suggestions for excerpting in magazines and newspapers, illustrations for promotional use, jacket blurb, special marketing suggestions.

10. *Reprint order* (from reprint and new edition manager to production department). Author, title, quantity, letterpress or offset, price, corrections or revisions, jackets (quantity, revisions), bind, ship, date needed.

III. *Design Department*

1. *Information for preliminary estimate* (before the contract is made, for preparation of a publication plan). Date, author, title, manuscript pages, quantity in thousands plus additional thousands, hardback or paperback, trim size, text characters per page, footnote characters per page, appendixes and bibliography characters per page, tables, illustrations (number, halftone or line, number of pages), type of jacket, stock for text, grade of cloth, stamping, quantity bound at one time, comments.

2. *Specifications sheet* (goes with designed manuscript to production department). Job number, title, author, editor, designer, date. Printer, quantity, trim page size, margins. Type for text, index, footnotes, running heads, folios, chapter openings, etc. Paper stock. Binding specifications. Jacket specifications. Specifications for illustrations, reproduction process, number of pieces of copy, paper stock, ink, style for legends.

IV. *Production Department*

1. *Production schedule.* Lists all books in production, alphabetically by title (revised and circulated weekly). With the author and title are given the initials of the editor, whether the schedule has been revised, job number, and date finished manuscript was received from author. The planned production schedule reads across on one line, and the actual dates are filled in below as each book progresses. A similar schedule is kept for binder's dies and jackets.

2. *Manufacturing cost estimate.* Most publishers transfer estimates from printers and binders to a uniform form. This helps the administration because all estimates are on the same form, so one knows where to look for standard information. It is desirable on the form to separate plant cost (items not affected by quantity) from production cost (items affected by quantity) and to show at the bottom the estimated plant cost of reprinting which (as seen in Chapter IV) should be kept in mind when determining the print order. Usually the form has several columns to provide space for cost estimates for various quantities, or for a basic quantity plus additional thousands.

3. *Circuit memo.* This memo is attached to proof coming from the printer. It lists in order each person who is to see the proof "on circuit," and each initials it and inserts the date when he sends it to the next person. The title, author, copyeditor, and job number are given at the top of the form.

V. *Marketing Department*

1. *Free copy order,* to the accounting department to ship free or examination copies.

2. *Review copy order form.* Lists review media by category. Publicity manager checks media to which review copies are to be sent. This form is completed and sent to the accounting department shortly before each book is delivered to the warehouse, so that review copies can go out immediately.

3. *Advertising schedules.* A semiannual seasonal program is developed for the space advertising planned for each book, with the space advertising arranged by media. The amount of space and cost are shown. A similar program is developed for direct mail, showing titles to be included in each catalogue or mailer, mailing lists to be used, scheduled mailing date, and probable cost. These programs are circu-

lated to all administrative staff, editors, and others.

4. *Itineraries of salesmen* are circulated to interested staff members.

5. *Order forms.* There are many varieties for the use of salesmen.

VI. *Accounting Department*

The many standard accounting forms that are used in accounting offices in many businesses are not included here. The balance sheet, operating statement, and cash-flow analysis are discussed in Chapter III. Here are a few additional accounting reports to other departments and to the general administration that may be helpful.

1. *Sales reports.* There are a variety of these, analyzed in different ways for different purposes. The by-title and by-subject reports are of particular interest to the editorial department. Most other sales reports are useful to the general administration or to the marketing manager. Sales analyses of various kinds are easy to get from a computerized accounting system, if the system is programmed to provide them. Sales reports may be monthly, weekly, or even daily for fast-moving titles.

a) by title or by author, alphabetically.

b) by subject category (politics, science, history, etc.).

c) by geographical area. Areas correspond to territories of salesmen, to areas in which advertising or sales efforts may be concentrated (e.g., the Midwest), or to states (particularly for adoption of textbooks).

d) foreign sales by country. This is a separate report because foreign sales are usually organized differently from domestic sales. Currency problems, censorship, or other difficulties may affect particular countries, and this can be seen in the foreign sales report.

e) by discount category.

f) by salesman.

g) by type of account, such as bookstore, library, wholesaler, and direct mail.

h) by account, in detail. This is of great interest to the marketing or sales manager and to salesmen.

i) by number of copies, hardback and paperback, categorized by subject. This is often accompanied by a calculation of the average net selling price.

j) backlist sales vs. current list, dollars and percent of total, with historical material for comparison.

k) analysis of returns by source, type of book, etc.

1) by price range, across the list and within subject categories. For example, rate of sale for paperbacks, for hardback books under $5.00, from $5.00 to $7.50, from $7.75 to $10.00, from $10.25 to $15.00, $15.25 or over.

2. *Studies of patterns of sale from publication date,* as discussed in Chapter IV. These may be by subject category, hardback or paperback, by price, etc. They are most useful if shown graphically as in Figures 10 and 14.

3. *Out-of-stock book report.* See the discussion on page 119 of Chapter IV. A monthly report of three-, six-, and nine-month notices should go to the reprint manager, along with a list of out-of-stock books and the accumulated back orders. The publisher will also want a notice of the percent of titles out of stock and a list of titles out of stock longer than a certain period or with more than a certain number of back orders, with explanations.

4. *Stock report.* This is often combined with the sales report, to show the number of copies of each book in the warehouse. The reprint manager must watch this report carefully. The report is also useful at the end of the fiscal year when it is necessary to write off dead stock, a sobering exercise.

FOR READING AND REFERENCE: A SELECTED LIST

I. *On Printing, Publishing, and Bookselling*

Anderson, Charles B., Joseph A. Duffy, and Jocelyn D. Kahn, *A Manual on Bookselling,* American Booksellers Association, distributed by Bowker, 1969. A publisher ought to know a lot about bookstores and how they work. This book is a mine of information.

Grannis, Chandler B., ed., *What Happens in Book Publishing,* second edition, Columbia University Press, 1967. The best all-around book on American book publishing. Essays by various experts cover all aspects. Anyone going into publishing should read it, and it is a refresher course for old hands.

Gross, Gerald, ed., *Publishers on Publishing,* Bowker, 1961. A compendium of writings by American publishers on publishing, from Daniel Macmillan in the mid-nineteenth century to Bennett Cerf in the mid-twentieth. Illuminating and amusing, giving some insight into the ways publishing has changed—and how it hasn't.

Hawes, Gene R., *To Advance Knowledge: A Handbook on American University Press Publishing,* The Association of American University Presses, 1967. This handbook includes some history, some "how to" sections, and many comments from press directors on aspects of university publishing. Useful reading for the publisher of specialized books.

Kerr, Chester, *A Report on American University Presses,* The Association of American University Presses, 1949. Supplement issued in 1956. A study of university presses sponsored by the American Council of Learned Societies, still the standard work, though to some extent supplanted by Hawes' *To Advance Knowledge.*

Lehman-Haupt, Hellmut, Lawrence Wroth, C. Silver, and C. Rollo,

The Book in America: A History of the Making and Selling and Collecting of Books in the United States, second edition, Bowker, 1951. This is the standard scholarly history.

Madison, Charles A., *A History of American Publishing,* McGraw-Hill, 1966. A compilation of the histories of publishing companies, mainly from "official" histories, brought together chronologically with little synthesis or critical comment. A useful source of facts about individual companies.

McMurtrie, Douglas, *The Book: The Story of Printing and Bookmaking,* third edition, Oxford University Press, 1943. An authoritative history of printing, with little attention to publishing.

Mott, Frank Luther, *Golden Multitudes: The Story of the Best Sellers in the United States,* Bowker, 1960. This book is essential background for the trade publisher, though it will not furnish a key to tomorrow's popular taste. Its substance is an important part of American cultural history.

Mumby, Frank Arthur, *Publishing and Bookselling: A History from the Earliest Times to the Present Day,* Bowker, 1930; revised in 1939 and 1954. The standard history of British publishing and bookselling, fascinating and delightful. It contains an extensive bibliography by William Fleet.

Publishers' Weekly, Bowker. The weekly journal of the book trade; essential reading for anyone in publishing.

Sheehan, Donald Henry, *This Was Publishing: A Chronicle of the Book Trade in the Gilded Age,* Indiana University Press, Bloomington, 1952. A lively history of American book publishing in the latter half of the nineteenth century.

Smith, Datus C., Jr., *A Guide to Book Publishing,* Bowker, 1966. An excellent introduction, somewhat simplified for the uninitiated reader. It is intended especially for publishers in the less developed countries, and is unique in its treatment of the special problems encountered in such areas.

Smith, Roger H., ed., *The American Reading Public: A Symposium from the Winter 1962 Issue of Daedelus,* Bowker, 1964. A collection of thoughtful essays by professors and publishers on the state of the book and book reading in America. It is more philosophic than most books about publishing, and deals also with such problems as the effects of book reviewing and of television.

Steinberg, S. H., *Five Hundred Years of Printing,* Penguin, 1955. An excellent short history, emphasizing the interrelations among printers, publishers, and the public.

Unwin, Sir Stanley, *The Truth About Publishing*, seventh revised edition, Macmillan, 1960. One of the half-dozen basic books about publishing, a course of instruction from one of the most successful British publishers. The American edition, though adapted, has a somewhat British flavor, and American publishers may prefer to read the British edition as an introduction to British publishing practices.

Williamson, Hugh, *Methods of Book Design: The Practice of an Industrial Craft*, Oxford, 1966 (second edition). An excellent comprehensive treatment of design and printing, combining aesthetic and technical aspects.

II. *On Style*

Bernstein, Theodore M., *The Careful Writer: A Modern Guide to English Usage*, Atheneum, 1965. By the former Assistant Managing Editor of the *New York Times*. A concise handbook, organized alphabetically. Also see Bernstein's *Watch Your Language* (Channel Press, 1958), compiled from his "Winners & Sinners" in the *Times*. Bernstein's incisive comments should sensitize any editor or writer.

Follett, Wilson, *Modern American Usage: A Guide*, Hill & Wang, 1966. America's closest rival to Fowler. Follett exhibits purity of taste, conservative but not pedantic. In addition to its alphabetical section, it contains several sensible essays on style, including an excellent section on the art and science of punctuation. A dose of Follett may be prescribed as an antidote to the permissive philosophy of Webster's "Third."

Fowler, H. W., *A Dictionary of Modern English Usage*, second edition revised by Sir Ernest Gowers, Oxford University Press, 1965. The incomparable compendium on usage, which all others seek to rival. Every copyeditor should have Fowler at his elbow, though the temptation to browse may be irresistible.

Graves, Robert, and Alan Hodge, *The Reader over Your Shoulder*, Macmillan, 1944. A daring book, and a delight for copyeditors. The authors rewrite the "greats" to show how they could have done it better—all explained by a set of principles, surprisingly convincing.

Manual of Style, 12th revised edition, Chicago University Press, 1969. The latest edition greatly improves one of an editor's most useful standard reference works. It is comprehensive, well-organized, well-indexed, authoritative, and beautifully printed. "Style" here means printer's and publisher's style. The *Manual* succeeds in its "aim to give clear and simple guidelines for preparing and editing copy."

McCartney, Eugene S., *Recurrent Maladies in Scholarly Writing,* University of Michigan Press, 1953. A delightful and informative book on a serious and important subject.

Montague, C. E., *A Writer's Notes on His Trade,* Pelican, 1930. Reflections on style. Except for this one, which I like very much but which is little known, I have excluded such books from this list.

Nicholson, Margaret, *A Dictionary of American-English Usage* (based on Fowler's *Modern English Usage*), Oxford University Press, 1957; also New American Library (paper), 1957. An adaptation, but most editors prefer the original Fowler.

Nicholson, Margaret, *A Practical Style Guide for Authors and Editors,* Holt, Rinehart, and Winston, 1967. A sensible short introduction, helpful to a beginner though not comprehensive enough for general use.

Partridge, Eric, *Usage and Abusage: A Guide to Good English,* revised edition 1957, Penguin Books, Baltimore, 1963. Intended as a supplement and complement to Fowler, with annotations of American usage by W. Cabell Greet. Partridge's love of the language shines through his sober comments. He combines elegance with concision.

Perkins, Maxwell E., *Editor to Author: The Letters of Maxwell E. Perkins,* Scribner's, 1950. The letters of one of the greatest American editors to Thomas Wolfe, Ernest Hemingway, F. Scott Fitzgerald, Erskine Caldwell, John Galsworthy, and others. An inspiring book, though not every editor can be a Perkins.

Strunk, William, Jr., and E. B. White, *The Elements of Style,* revised edition, Macmillan, 1959. Every writer and every editor ought to read this little book—and follow its advice.

Webster's New Collegiate Dictionary, latest edition, G. & C. Merriam Co., Springfield, Mass. The most popular desk dictionary, based on the authoritative *Webster's New International Dictionary.* Editions of the *Collegiate* based on the Second Edition of the *New International* contain a section on Punctuation that is the best available short course on good practice in formal writing—very useful for copyeditors. Unfortunately *Collegiate* editions based on the Third Edition of the *New International* contain a new section on Punctuation, based largely on the spoken language, which is usful at best only for informal writing. Punctuation based on speech assumes that the reader reads with his lips, and it fails to provide structural information that may be necessary for clarity and that in any case helps the rapid reader.

Webster's New International Dictionary (Unabridged), Third Edition, G. & C. Merriam Co., Springfield, Mass. This is the best unabridged dictionary of American English, an essential reference for every editor. The Third Edition caused an outcry among editors and writers because it abandoned many of the helpful practices of the Second, especially the practice of giving the "preferred" usage. Thus it refused responsibility for setting standards of good usage and limited itself to reporting, including without warning many usages usually regarded as substandard. It is nevertheless an excellent dictionary, but the weight of its authority will help substandard usages to gain acceptance, with a resulting loss of clarity and precision in our language.

III. *Reference Works on Books and the Book Trade*

The American Book Trade Directory, biennial, Bowker. A directory of American publishers, booksellers, antiquarians, wholesalers, auctioneers, book clubs, book trade periodicals, exporters and importers, and publishers and booksellers in Great Britain and Canada.

Bogsch, Arpad, *The Law of Copyright under the Universal Convention,* Bowker, 1964.

The Book Buyer's Handbook, annual, American Booksellers' Association. Trade terms of all publishers.

Books in Print (U.S.A.), annual, Bowker. By title and by author. See also *Subject Guide to Books in Print,* annual, Bowker; and *Paperbound Books in Print* (U.S.A.), monthly, Bowker.

The Bowker Annual of Library and Book Trade Information, Bowker. Library and book-trade statistics, library standards, legislation and grants, education and manpower, library and book-trade associations and committees, events, prizes, and financial information.

Copyright Law of the U.S.A., latest printing, Government Printing Office, Washington, D.C. The basic law on which the publishing industry is built. The G.P.O. pamphlet also contains copyright treaties and conventions to which the United States is a party, with lists of other signatories.

Directory of Newspapers and Periodicals, annual, N. W. Ayer, Philadelphia.

General Information on Copyright, Circular 1 of The Copyright Office, Government Printing Office, Washington, D.C. A good, short summary. See also Circular 38A on *International Copyright Relations*, Circular 38B on *Berne Union Member Countries*, and Circular 38C on *Universal Copyright Convention—Accessions and Ratifications*.

Graves, Eileen C., ed., *Ulrich's International Periodicals Directory*, annual, Bowker.

International Literary Market Place, latest edition, Bowker. A directory similar to *The Literary Market Place*.

The Literary Market Place, annual, Bowker. A directory of publishers, book clubs, agents, associations, manufacturers, magazines, newspapers, radio, TV, translators, and various other services.

Nicholson, Margaret, *A Manual of Copyright Practice for Writers, Publishers, and Agents*, Oxford University Press, latest edition. A clear explanation of the U.S. law of literary property, including the Universal Copyright Convention. It deals with books, magazines, and other forms of publication, and contains a helpful section of questions and answers.

Melcher, Daniel, and Nancy Larrick, *The Printing and Promotion Handbook*, third edition, McGraw-Hill, 1966. A unique guide to printing technology and advertising and promotion techniques, arranged alphabetically.

Pilpel, Harriet F., and Morton D. Goldberg, *Copyright Guide*, second edition, Bowker, 1963. A reliable brief guide, concise and clear.

Pollock, Muriel, ed., *Publishers' Trade List Annual*, Bowker. A collection in four volumes of the trade lists of all American publishers.

INDEX